THE BOOK OF APHORISMS

The Book of Aphorisms

Being a translation of
Kitāb al-Ḥikam

❖

Ibn ʿAṭāʾillāh al-Iskandarī

Translated by
Muhammed Nafih Wafy

Islamic Book Trust
Kuala Lumpur

Reprint 2018
Islamic Book Trust
607 Mutiara Majestic
Jalan Othman
46000 Petaling Jaya
Selangor, Malaysia
www.ibtbooks.com

Islamic Book Trust is affiliated with The Other Press.

Perpustakaan Negara Malaysia   Cataloguing-in-Publication Data

Ibn 'Ata' Allah, Aḥmad ibn Muḥammad, 1309
    The book of aphorisms / Ibn 'Ata'illah al-Iskandari ; translated by
    Muhammed Nafih Wafy.
    ISBN 978-967-5062-61-2
    1. Sufism--Early works to 1800.
    I. Muhammed Nafih Wafy. II. Title.
    297.4

Printed by
SS Graphic Printers (M) Sdn. Bhd.
Lot 7 & 8, Jalan TIB 3
Taman Industri Bolton
68100 Batu Caves, Selangor

Contents

Introduction

Aḥmad ibn Muḥammad ibn Aṭā'illāh al-Iskandarī was a great Sufi master and jurisprudence scholar who was born into a distinguished family of religious scholars in Alexandria in the thirteenth century (7 AH), when Egypt was ruled by Mamlūks. He started his education as a disciple of Abū al-Ḥasan al-Abyārī, a famous Mālikī jurist, and studied under some of the best and most illustrious teachers of Alexandria at the time. He was well versed in all disciplines of traditional Islamic knowledge and became a distinguished Mālikī scholar. Ibn ʿAṭā'illāh was initially not drawn to Sufism in spite of his father's attachment to the great Sufi Shaykh Abū al-Ḥasan al-Shādhilī, the founder of the Shādhilī Sufi order. After a stint as a teacher and preacher in Alexandria, he moved to Cairo where he taught jurisprudence, Ḥadīth and Taṣawwuf at al-Azhar Mosque and Manṣūriyyah *madrasah* as well as privately to his disciples. A large number of Islamic scholars of the time including the Shāfiʿī jurists Taqī al-Dīn al-Subkī and Imam al-Qarāfī were his disciples.

It was his meeting with Abū al-ʿAbbās al-Mursī, the second shaykh of Shādhlī Sufi order, that precipitated a major shift in his life. Recalling his first conversation with al-Mursī, he later said that the Shaykh had advised him on how to deal with the four states in a man's life: blessing, trial, obedience and disobedience. When he complained of some anxieties gnawing at him, the Shaykh advised him: "If you are blessed, what Allah requires of you is thankfulness. If you are tried, what Allah requires of you is patience. If you are obedient, what Allah requires of you is your contemplating His blessings upon you. If you are disobedient, then what Allah requires of you is your asking for forgiveness." After his first conversation with al-Mursī, Ibn 'Aṭā'illāh felt that his worries and grief were like a garment that had been taken off.

Then he became a devoted disciple of al-Mursī. His association with the Shaykh for twelve years saw his development as a great Sufi master capable of guiding and teaching others. Besides a scholar of great erudition and undoubted originality, Ibn 'Aṭā'illāh became an authority on both the Sufi path and Islamic Law.

He became widely respected and honoured in Cairo among all sections of people, including the high echelons of the ruling dynasty. His advice and suggestions were held in high regard by the Mamlūk sultans. He was also influential in the Mamlūk court, and used to counsel Sultan al-Manṣūr on religious matters.

He wrote the first systematic treatise on *dhikr*, titled *The Key to Salvation: A Sufi Manual of Invocation (Miftāḥ al-Falāḥ)*. This was followed by his magnum opus, *Kitāb al-Ḥikam* (The Book of Aphorisms), and numerous other works aimed at guiding people on the right path to spiritual salvation.

The writing of *Ḥikam*, arguably his most important work, marked his development as a Sufi master in his own right. Meanwhile, after the demise of al-Mursī he was appointed as the great master of the Shādhiliyyah order, which expanded from Morocco and spread throughout North Africa and beyond.

His other important works are *al-Qaṣd al-Mujarrad fī Maʿrifah al-Ism al-Mufrad* (The Pure Goal Concerning Knowledge of the Unique Name), *Tāj al-ʿArūs al-Ḥāwī li Tahdhīb al-Nufūs* (The Bride's Crown Containing the Discipline of Souls), *ʿUnwān al-Tawfīq fī Ādāb al-Ṭarīq* (The Sign of Success Concerning the Discipline of the Path), *Laṭāʾif al-Minan fī Manāqib Abī al-ʿAbbās al-Mursī wa Shaykhih Abī al-Ḥasan* (The Subtle Blessings of the Commendable Acts of Abū al-ʿAbbās al-Mursī and His Shaykh Abū al-Ḥasan al-Shādhilī).

He influenced a great number of people, including scholars, rulers and laymen, who came to him for spiritual advice and solace. He straddled at ease the professional life as a teacher of Mālikī jurisprudence in various public institutions and mosques in Cairo and his life as a spiritual master of the Shādhilī order imparting spiritual light to hundreds of his disciples. He was the first to systematise the Shādhilī order's doctrines and to record the biographies of its founder, Abū al-Ḥasan al-Shādhilī, and his successor, Abū al-ʿAbbās al-Mursī.

Even his contemporary Ibn Taymiyyah, who cast aspersion on some of the Sufis at the time and had differences with Ibn ʿAṭāʾillāh on several issues, described him as a man of scrupulous piety, abundant learning, integrity and truthfulness in speech. During a historic debate between these two eminent scholars of the time at al-Azhar Mosque, Ibn Taymiyyah said, "I bear witness that I have seen no one like you either in Egypt or in Syria who loves Allah more, is more self-effacing in Him and is more obedient in carrying out what He has commanded and in refraining from what He has forbidden." This complement from Ibn Taymiyyah is enough to prove the respect and admiration he earned from his contemporaries cutting across all divides.

Shaykh Ibn 'Atā'illāh died at the age of 60 in November 1309 at al-Manṣūriyyah *madrasah*. He was laid to rest at Qarāfah Cemetery in Cairo after a funeral procession attended by a large number of people.

❖

Kitāb al-Ḥikam is a slender mystic classic which enjoys a universal reputation as the jewel in the crown of Sufi literature. The book is a collection of 261 Sufi aphorisms (some counted it 264) containing precise, contemplative reflections on man's relations with his Creator. It is designed as a manual of spiritual development aimed at guiding and instructing spiritual aspirants and pursuers. Purely based on the teachings of the noble Qur'an and the sayings of Prophet Muḥammad (ṣ), the book provides training to fulfil the objectives of sublime servanthood in human life through developing a deep relation with the Almighty God.

It explains the way to live Islam both outwardly and inwardly and guides people towards the perfection of good character and spiritual realisation. Most of the aphorisms are written in a conversational format addressing a second person, obviously the spiritual aspirant.

The *Ḥikam* was evidently dictated by the Shaykh to one of his disciples, who was none other than Taqī al-Dīn al-Subkī, who later handed it over to Shādhilī master Aḥmad Zarrūq.

As a unique and beautiful work written in a meditative language and inimitable style, *Ḥikam* attracted universal Muslim approval from his own time up to the present day. A combination of profound spiritual teachings, real charm of language, forcefulness of expression and intensity of conviction makes *Ḥikam* certainly the most appealing of Ibn 'Atā'illāh's books to later generations of Muslims.

Over a period, *Ḥikam* has been the object of numerous commentaries by eminent scholars. Some of the famous commentators are Shaykh Muḥammad ibn Ibrāhīm (Ibn 'Abbād al-Rundī), Shaykh al-Islām 'Abdullāh al-Sharqāwī, Shaykh Aḥmad Zarrūq, founder of the Zarrūqiyyah Sufi order, and Aḥmad ibn 'Ajībah. Most recently, a four-volume commentary of the *Ḥikam* was written by modern scholar Muḥammad Sa'īd Ramāḍān al-Būṭī.

In the earlier chapters, the book delves into the profound meaning of monotheism and examines the subtlest ways of idolatry and polytheism that hinder one's true spiritual development. This is followed by aphorisms related to improving human character and achieving mental purification. The final part of the book deals with the obligations and requirements of a true spiritual journey.

The second section of the book is made up of four letters (also known as four treatises) written by Shaykh Ibn 'Aṭā'illāh in response to questions of some of his disciples. They contain his mystical and philosophical deliberations and reflections on man's relation to God and his profound observations on some Qur'anic verses and sayings of the Prophet.

The book ends with intimate discourses (*al-Munājāt al-Ilāhiyyah*). They are intimate supplications reflecting total submission to God. Most of them are coined by the Shaykh combining the supplications in the Qur'an, Ḥadīth and prayers of the Companions, while some others are attributed to the Prophet's grandson al-Ḥasan ibn 'Alī.

Both the four treatises and intimate discourses form an organic part of the whole.

1

Trust in God

Losing hope when a slippage occurs is a sign of relying too much on (one's own) deeds.

An ordinary servant of Allah depends on his deeds, including his prayers and supplications, to enter Paradise and escape Allah's punishment whereas a spiritual aspirant (*murīd*) takes his deeds as a means to reach Allah. But an enlightened servant (gnostic or *'ārif*) will never trust or depend on his deeds. He will neither rejoice over a good thing he did, nor regret a fault that happened to him, because he has dedicated himself to Allah, so that his doing or not-doing is no more important for him.

Since people belonging to the first and second category ascribe their success or failure to their deeds, they lose hope when they commit a mistake; but those who belong to the third category are so preoccupied with Allah that they are not concerned about the value of their deeds.

Since he does not want his selfish motives to dilute the quality of his worship, the enlightened servant makes Allah the pivot of whatever he does. If achieving any selfish interest, even if it be entering Paradise, becomes the objective of worship, Allah will cease to become the first priority. With the focus shifting from Allah to something lesser, such as self, worship loses much of its sheen and becomes a substandard means to scrape through the test of Allah.

If a man rejoices over a good thing he did, it means he is furtively impressed by his calibre and skills, which he believes enabled him to do that; but his pleasure is totally misplaced because he is unable to do that without Allah's blessings. If he loses hope when he commits a mistake, it also shows that he attaches too much importance to his deeds. When he himself becomes the focus of his deeds, His worship hardly serves the purpose demanded of it. One who considers each supplication a means to improve the prospect of winning an individual achievement and each mistake as an opportunity squandered, will mourn one's mistakes as if one were responsible for them and were to pay the penalty for them.

Your aspiring for isolation when Allah puts you among the causes (of everyday living) is a covert ambition; and your aspiring for the causes (of everyday living) when Allah prefers isolation for you is a collapse from exalted steadfastness.

Circumstances of life may differ from person to person. Allah sends each and every person with different representations to fill different slots. From a saint to a layman, everybody has his own distinct and unique role to perform. One has to do justice to one's duties and to be true to one's circumstances. Despite being one of the distinguished prophets, Moses was unable to live like Khaḍir; and it was unbecoming of Khaḍir to come down to the level of Moses. Each person has his own respective areas to concentrate on and to prove his mettle.

As nobody is able to decide the time and place of his birth, the father and mother who gave birth to him, the race and the gender he belongs to, nobody has the right to ask for a change in the circumstances of his life. The servant is asked to prove himself in whatever circumstances he is asked to live in. If he asks for a better situation, it means he failed to prove his servant-hood in the present situation. If he aspires to become a saint when Allah decided to test him as an ordinary man, his aspiration betrays his incapability to succeed the test as an ordinary man. And if he wants to become an ordinary man when Allah decided to test him as a saint, he fails to rise up to the expectation. While soliciting a change in the circumstances of life, he is trying to poke his nose into Allah's business.

Predestination

Intentions cannot intrude the walls of preordained things.

The human willpower is but a means to the unfurling of predestined divine decree. Though man is endowed with freewill, which enables him to mould his destiny, he is never authorised to challenge the divine diktats. When his hard work bears fruit, he cannot misread it as a victory of his determination against divine odds. Allah was using his determination as a means to change his destiny.

Indifference to material riches

Don't bother to think (about your worldly fortunes). Why do you undertake to do what someone else has already done on your behalf.

Your striving for what has already been offered to you
and your negligence in what is demanded of you show
the deterioration of your insight.

Attaching too much importance to procuring material gains is contrary to the objectives of man's creation and to the requirements of his existence. Since worshiping Allah is the intention behind man's creation and the spirit of his covenant with Him, he is obliged to concentrate more on fulfilling his accord rather than worrying about his material life. Any deviation or shift of focus from the main objective of life is caused by a distorted perception which makes him too myopic to understand his mission on the earth. While his Creator and Cherisher is in charge of his protection, why is he so worried about it? His concerns about the worldly life betray his lack of confidence in his Creator and his suspicion about His blessings. It's very strange that man is oblivious of his responsibilities while he is still in the pursuit of what he has already been offered.

Allah knows what is best for the servant

Don't let the delay in getting the gift (answer), despite
your persistent appeal, drive you to despair. For He
has offered to reply to (your appeals) in a way He
chooses for you rather than in a way you choose for
yourself, and at a time He desires rather than at a
time you desire.

If you insist on getting instant responses for your prayers, it shows your impatience and your incapability to understand the way, manner and method of His responses. He maybe delaying the answer to give it in an appropriate way and at an appropriate time. Since you do not know what is good for you today and what will be good for you tomorrow and even what was good for you in the past, let Him decide on the time and manner of the answer. By showing frustration and impatience at not getting what you aspired, you are really doing an injustice to yourself.

Don't let the non-fulfilment of a promise, even if the time of its fulfilment has been specified, make you suspicious of the promise, as it may obscure your intellect and extinguish your inner light.

The delay in the fulfilment of a divine promise coming true does not mean the promise will never be fulfilled. Only Allah knows the opportune time for fulfilling His promise. While Allah knows better when His promise should be fulfilled, why does the servant grow apprehensive about its non-fulfilled What is demanded of him is to let Allah fulfil it as and when its time comes. If he becomes doubtful about it, it will adversely affect his optimism and intellectual capabilities and will diminish the power of his inner light.

When Allah unfolds a realm of knowledge for you, get rid of the feeling that you are not qualified for that in terms of deeds. He opened up that for you because He wanted to make Himself known to you. Don't you know that the knowledge was His presentation for you, while the deeds were yours for Him and, of course, your presentation will be zilch compared to that of Him.

If Allah decides to bless the servant with knowledge of Him, then there is no point in his assessment that his deeds were not sufficient for deserving such a blessing. For no reciprocation on his part will be enough to measure up to what He has bestowed on him. The servant's anxiety over not being able to give back through his deeds is totally misplaced. His knowledge of Allah will be more powerful than his deeds in defining the course of his life.

What Allah prefers for the servant must be better than what he prefers for himself. If Allah chooses for him the way of knowledge rather than that of deeds, he need not be afraid of missing the opportunities for performing good deeds and thereby losing rewards in the hereafter. Who can assure him that the way of deeds will be better? How can he predict that all his deeds will be secure from defects and will be worth rewarding at the end of the day? How can he foretell that his performance will be impeccable in another track of life about which he has only some fictitious ideas and obscured calculations?

Inspiration shows the way

Actions differ according to the differences in the circumstances of inspiration.

An inner motivation persuades an individual for doing a particular action. The action differs from individual to individual according to the differences in this motivation. Therefore, actions are but the outward manifestations of an internal process.

Actions are but motionless forms, and their spirit (and sustenance) lies in the presence of a committed heart within.

Commitment (*ikhlāṣ*) also differs from person to person. If it's only purging the action of the traces of pride and smugness in usual cases, it requires the complete depersonalisation through the extinction of self in the case of a saint. However, unaccompanied by commitment, actions are lifeless and devoid of any significance.

No shortcut to success

Bury your existence in the ground of insignificance because what sprouts out of an unburied seed will not yield good results.

The success achieved without humility will be short-lived. Even for a seed to grow as a tree, to flower and to fruit it has to bury itself in the soil. From the darkness of the earth, it sprouts forth to become a tree of significance. Likewise, for a man to achieve the true success demanded of his existence, he has to bury his inclination for reputation.

There is no shortcut to achieve the eventual success. One has to take the natural course for getting to the destination. If one succumbs to the temptation to pursue the shortcuts in order to be famous, it will ultimately lead to one's failure and to the total catastrophe of one's mission.

Seclusion and meditation

Nothing will be as beneficial to the heart as seclusion wherein it enters the domain of meditation.

Loneliness will create in the mind an atmosphere conducive to meditation. When the mind is engaged in worldly concerns, it is not likely to reflect on Allah. Thought, if it is fully detached from other personal preoccupations, is a powerful vehicle capable of leading man to the presence of Allah. For thought to enter the level of meditation, it has to be fully independent and undisturbed by meaningless concerns.

Cleansing the heart of blemishes

How can a heart be illuminated when its mirror reflects worldly figures only? Or how can it journey to Allah, manacled with its passions? Or how can it crave for entering the presence of Allah without being cleansed of the blemishes of its forgetfulness? Or how can it understand the subtle nuances of mysteries, while it has yet to repent of its wrongdoings?

The heart will lose its transparency and brightness if it reflects only worldly figures. Passions and worldly concerns create obstacles in front of the heart on its way to Allah. If it continues to lose in its oblivion, it is not likely to wake up to the realities. Only a heart that is vigilant and alert to sins can tread the difficult path to salvation.

The omnipresence of divine light

The whole universe would have been enveloped in darkness had it not been lighted up by His manifestation. So, if one fails to witness Him in, with, before or after the universe, he misses the presence of the lights. That is, the clouds of worldly things veil the suns of knowledge.

It is the presence of Allah that illuminated the whole universe. Therefore, one who fails to notice even a shred of this divine light cannot perceive divine presence anywhere in the world. It means that some clouds have denied to man the sight of knowledge's mercury, so that he was left in utter darkness, unable to see the light of the day.

That He veils you from Himself with what has no real existence alongside Him is an indication of His omnipotence.

How can it be imagined that something may veil Him while He made everything visible? How can it be imagined that something may veil Him while He is visible with everything? How can it be imagined that something may veil Him while He is visible in everything? How can it be imagined that something may veil Him while He is visible to everything? How can it be imagined that something may veil Him while He was visible before everything came into existence? How can it be imagined that something may veil Him while He is more visible than anything else? How can it be imagined that something may veil Him while He is the One and nothing else exists alongside Him?

How can it be imagined that something may veil Him while He is closer to you than anything else? How can it be imagined that something may veil Him while had it not been for Him nothing would have been existent?

Is it strange that being can appear in non-being and the ephemeral can coexist with one for whom eternity is an attribute.

Anything that veils Allah has no real existence at all, because before Allah made it visible, it was non-existent. It means nothing that seems to veil Allah can really do so. If everything in this universe indicates Allah's presence and depends on Him for its existence, it is totally absurd to say that something can hide Him. Besides, for everything Allah's presence is very essential and more important than the existence of anything else.

2

How to deal with time

It's sheer stupidity to seek to introduce in a given time what Allah has not manifested in it.

Only Allah knows what is better for the servant. Since a servant cannot predict what is good and what is bad for himself, he should not seek a better situation. He is requested to make better use of whatever situation is given to him rather than asking for a better situation. The servant becomes more sincere and honest if he works for the master in whatever situation he was asked to work without asking for a change in the situation of the work. If he believes that he can become more productive and efficient in a different situation, it is tantamount to believing that he knows better than Allah what situation is better for him.

To postpone deeds until leisure time comes is one of the frivolities of the mind.

It is stupid to postpone your duties till when you are free. Each moment requires its own share of duties from you. If you postpone your duties of this time to an imagined free time in the future, what will you do with your duties in the future? Nobody is entitled to claim what he will do or will not do in a given time in the future.

> *Do not ask Him to take you out of a situation so that you will be employed in a different situation. For had He intended so, He would have employed you in it even without changing your circumstances.*

Asking for a situation other than what Allah has selected for you reveals your disbelief in Allah's ability to make a suitable choice for you. How can a sincere servant disbelieve Allah's destiny for him?

Inner voice

> *No sooner did a determined initiate want to stop at a particular revelation than an inner voice of reality called out to him: "What you are looking for is still ahead of you." And no sooner did the veneer of the worldly things allure him than their inner realities called out to him: We are but tricksters so beware of being misled.*

No temporary destination could mislead a determined spiritual aspirant. Whenever he tends to stop his journey there, he will be advised by an inner voice to proceed. Nor worldly charm could delude him because he is always guided by the inner realities. Those who are inspired by the inner realities will not be allured by false landmarks and directions.

Four types of request

> *If you request Him it means you are suspicious about Him; if you seek Him it means you are absent from*

Him. If you seek someone else it means you are unabashed by (what you are doing to) Him; if you request to someone else it means you are distant from Him.

There are four different stages of digression that a servant may go through on the basis of his request: If the servant requests something from Allah, it means he suspects Allah's knowledge about his needs. If he has to seek Him, it means he is not beside Him. If he seeks someone else, it means he is not ashamed of doing so. If he requests someone else, it means he is still far from Allah.

There is not a single exhalation by you that is not predestined by Him.

Each action of the servant, including his exhalation and inhalation, is predestined by Allah. His share of obedience or sin in each molecule of time was preordained by Him. Therefore, he cannot ignore the value of each second in life and its contribution towards his eternal success.

Procrastination

Do not wait to be free of others, because it may hamper your attentiveness to Him in that state He has assigned to you.

Life is full of alterities and vicissitudes. It is absurd to wait for a day without alterities to carry out one's duties. Such a waiting is a sinful procrastination that makes the individual oblivious of his faculties spoiling all his skills in the expectation of something that may never come. He cannot understand the importance of his present situation unless he explores all its potentials and possibilities. If he finds a situation difficult, it does not mean Allah has created a difficult situation for him; but it means he is not able to make a virtue of necessity and to emerge stronger and more successful in life.

✿

Do not consider the existence of grief strange as long as you live in this world. For whatever it reflects is its essential attributes and characteristic features.

The true aspirant cannot consider anything, including grief, a serious impediment in the course of his pursuit. He knows well that he has to sacrifice many worldly gains and riches to achieve his ultimate goal.

✿

Divine patronage

No pursuit you make with the help of your Lord will stagnate, while all pursuits you make on your own will not be that easy.

Without Allah's help and support, no pursuit will be successful. The guidance and patronage of Allah will relieve the aspirant of all troubles and anxieties.

✿

The beginning informs the end

Resorting to Allah in the very beginning is a symbol of ultimate success.

An enterprise oriented towards and pivoted around Allah from the beginning itself is bound to be successful.

✿

If one's beginning was illuminated, one's end will also be illuminated.

There are two stages in the journey of an initiate (*sālik*) to Allah: the beginning stage and the concluding or final stage. If one sweats over achieving spiritual enlightenment from the very early stage of one's journey, one's mind and body will be trained and streamlined in a way that expedites one's spiritual illumination. It helps him purify himself and facilitate the process. The more careful and hardworking he is in the beginning, the more successful and rewarding will be the enterprise he ventures into.

Manifestation of light

Whatever is reserved in the secret interiors (of one's heart) will be visible through (one's) external appearance.

The light of knowledge and wisdom that illuminates the heart of a servant cannot help finding an outlet to manifest itself. If one's mind is devoted to Allah, one's body will follow suit. As the Messenger of Allah (ṣ) has aptly put it, "if his heart is pious, his limbs will also be pious."

Inference starts from Him

What a difference between those who begin their inference from Allah as evidence and those who proceed to Allah from other evidences. Those who consider him the evidence can exactly define the truth and confirm the point with reference to its roots. The

method of seeking Him from other evidences betrays
an absence of union with Him. It makes Him virtually
absent till proved with evidences and distant till
accessed by other indications (His creatures).

One who starts the inference from the truth will be more
conclusive in one's assertions and claims, while one who starts
it from assumptions will be more fallible and circumspect in
one's claims. In the second method, the truth will be absent
till the seeker proves it, while in the first method all other
arguments should germinate from the truth. Therefore, the
servant is advised to start his inference from Allah as the first
point rather than beginning from other evidences to Him. No
evidence of Allah is as strong as Him and nothing can be so
strong an evidence of itself as Allah.

Journey to Allah

Those who have already reached Him belong to
the "let him who has abundance spend out of his
abundance" group, while those who are still on a
journey to Him belong to "whoever has his means of
subsistence straitened to him" group.

The Qur'anic reference "Let him who has abundance
spend out of his abundance" (65:7) is used as an attribute
of those who have already reached Allah; and the second
reference "and the man whose resources are restricted, let him
spend according to what Allah has given him" (65:7) is used
as an attribute of those who are still on a journey to Him. The
Qur'anic phrases quoted do not have a direct relation with
the context. But they are employed as two strong metaphors
to drive home a powerful message. The first group is equated

with the well-to-do people using a Qur'anic phrase which refers to affluent people's charity. It means those who have reached Allah have an abundance of information at their disposal and will have no shortage of resources. The second group is equated to the poor using the subsequent Qur'anic reference to those who do not have enough money to spend. It means those who are still on a journey to Him always suffer from shortage of resources and other means.

Those who journey to Him are guided by the lights in their directions whereas those who have already reached Him are in front of the lights. The former belongs to the lights whereas the lights belong to the latter, who belongs only to Him. "Say, 'Allah!' Then leave them to plunge in vain discourse and trifling" (Qur'an, 6:91).

The author explains another difference between those who are voyaging to Him and those who have already reached Him. While the former is being guided by the lights, the latter is in front of the lights. How can those who are always in the presence of the lights be equal to those who are being led by the lights but are unable to feel or perceive them?

3

Self-evaluation

*To be on the lookout for the deficiencies inherent in
your self is better than bothering about transcendental
things.*

An aspirant is advised to track and mend his deficiencies
rather than sparing time and effort to find out transcendental
realities. He is obliged to cleanse himself of all defects and
shortcomings. This is a duty which he carries out to please
his master whereas searching for transcendental realities is
an act which serves his own selfish interests. He indulges in
the former to please his Master, while the latter is a means to
promote his ambitions.

Nothing can veil Him

*It is not the Real who is veiled from you but rather you
who are veiled from seeing Him. If anything seeks to
veil Him, He will cover it. If He were ever covered, that
would be a restriction for His existence; the restricted is
always subject to the restriction. "He is the Irresistible,*

(watching) from above over His worshippers" (Qur'an, 6:18).

Nothing can hide or restrict Allah. If Allah is veiled or restricted by something, it means He is subject to veils and restrictions. It is our shortcomings and limitations that make Allah imperceptible to our eyes. Therefore, in order to reach Allah, we are asked to remedy our deficiencies instead of trying in vain to transcend the barriers that supposedly demarcate the divine realm.

Weeding out

Divest yourself of all human attributes that are not in harmony with your servanthood so that you can be responsive to the call of Allah and closer to His presence.

The perfection of an individual's personality lies in acquiring complete servanthood. To facilitate this perfection, he ought to weed out all his human traits that are not compatible with servanthood, such as arrogance, dishonesty, etc. Only those who achieved this level of perfection can be responsive to the call of Allah.

If one allows these traits to grow unchecked, they will adversely affect the health and growth of one's personality. If these bad traits are allowed a free rein, they will mar the soul's prospects of getting closer to Allah.

Self-satisfaction and self-dissatisfaction

All types of disobedience and negligence can be traced to self-satisfaction, while all sorts of obedience, vigilance and righteousness stem from self dissatisfaction. To associate with an ignorant man who is dissatisfied with himself is preferable to associating with a self-assured scholar. For a self-satisfied scholar does not have true knowledge, and an unlearned man who is not satisfied with himself is not really ignorant.

Self-satisfaction is the basis of all sorts of disobedience and negligence. Complacency signifies a state of stagnation which blocks the individual's mental and spiritual growth. At this stage, he is governed by certain trivial passions which make him blind to his real situation and status as a servant and create in him bigotry and arrogance. He will be less interested in improving himself and more concerned about projecting himself.

Self-dissatisfaction makes the individual more humble, cautious and vigilant and prompts him to explore new ways and means of improvement. Those who are not satisfied with themselves will not be self-centric or self-oriented. They always keep a spirit of dynamism and believe that there is more room for improvement.

Three phases of development

The ray of intellect helps you experience His proximity to you. The eye of intellect helps you experience your non-existence because of His existence. The truth of intellect helps you experience His existence only, irrespective of your existence or non-existence.

The author succinctly refers to three stages of development in a spiritual aspirant's pursuit. He who is blessed with the rays of intellectual light will experience nearness to Allah.

In this stage, the individual will witness the divine presence with the radiance of intellect. He who is blessed with the eyes of the intellectual light will experience his existence being outshone by the existence of Allah. In this stage, the individual will contemplate the divine presence with the radiance of knowledge. He who is blessed with the truth of the intellectual light will experience Allah's existence, not bothered about his existence or non-existence. In this stage, the individual will contemplate the divine presence with the light of truth.

In the third stage, the spiritual light will fully encompass the individual, so that he will not perceive anything except for Allah.

"Allah was, and there was nothing with Him, and He is now as He was."

When Allah's existence is manifest in its reality, everything becomes insignificant and irrelevant.

4

Focus on Him

Let not the focus of your aspiration deviate from Him,
because no hope can outstrip the Generous.

The spiritual initiate can never shift his focus from Allah.
If Allah, the Most Generous, is his only anchor and cherisher,
how can he pin his hope and faith on someone else?

Appeal to none but Him to dispose of a problem that
He Himself has brought about. For how can someone
else remove what He has imposed? How can one who
is unable to meet one's own needs do it for someone
else?

Only Allah can relieve you of a pressing need which He
Himself has created. If Allah is the source of all visitations and
disasters, how can you ask for help someone else who is unable
to solve his own problems?

If His good attributes are not sufficient for you to
improve your impression of Him, let the way He treats
you improve your impression of Him. For He has

habituated you to good things only and conferred on
you nothing but His bounties.

Allah's nature and attributes are good enough to improve
one's impression of Him. But if you are unable to form your
opinion and impression of Allah by seeing His attributes only,
the way He treats you should make you reflect on His bounties
and favours. Allah has bestowed only good things on His
servants.

It is all the more surprising to see one flee from where
there is no escape and search for what is ephemeral.
"Truly it is not their eyes that are blind, but their
hearts which are in their breasts" (Qur'an, 22:46).

There is no escape from Allah and nobody can flee from
Allah. Whoever runs away from Allah will end up in His own
capture. It is surprising to see man pursuing worldly gains,
which are transient and ephemeral, at the expense of what is
enduring and eternal.

Do not travel from creature to creature as if you were
a donkey in the mill, its destination always the starting
point itself. You had better travel from creatures to
the Creator. "Truly it is not their eyes that are blind,
but their hearts, which are in their breasts" (Qur'an,
22:46). If you are wise enough, try to ponder over what
the Prophet (ṣ) said, "Therefore, he whose migration is
for Allah and His Messenger, then his migration is for
Allah and His Messenger; and he whose migration is
for worldly gain or marriage with a woman, then his
migration is for that which he flees to."

For a thought to become dynamic, it has to move from the narrow constraints of this world to the broad divine realm. One whose thoughts always circle around this world and its concerns is really stuck in a whirlpool of stagnant waters. His thoughts are static as they will never reach a destination, just like a donkey which will never have a new destination. Human thought that is lost in such a futile exercise is like stagnant water, which neither moves nor has fountains to replenish it.

The famous saying of the Prophet (ṣ) about migration, quoted by the author makes it unequivocally clear that the life of the faithful is not of any use if it is not fully oriented to Allah, both in purpose and in intention. If the intention behind an act is not fully cleansed of personal interests and ambitions, it will not be accepted by Allah, however laborious the task undertaken maybe.

5

Friendship

Do not associate with anyone whose circumstances do not awaken you and whose words do not guide you to Allah.

Situations and surroundings have a crucial role in moulding one's character and mind's orientation. Therefore, the faithful should be very discreet about choosing his companions because they play a decisive role in his future life. As the old adage says, discretion is the better part of valour.

The concept of friendship can be taken in a broader perspective. All types of association in life, including family relations, political and social activities, education and professional careers come within the purview of friendship.

One should display discretion not only in the selection of friends and spouses but also in deciding what books to read, media programmes to watch, tourist destinations to visit and other modes of association in life.

The faithful are advised to associate only with things, situation and people whose presence and words can inspire him to Allah.

*If you are bad, your association with one who is worse
will show you your own virtues (in good light).*

The faithful person should recognise his good qualities
and spiritual dispositions so that he can understand his
greatness compared to others and try to promote them.

It is the mind that counts

*Hardly scarce are deeds emanating from an ascetic
mind and hardly abundant are deeds originating from
an avaricious mind.*

The supplication of an ascetic is more meaningful
because he performs it understanding its real meaning and
spirit. The hedonist, or one whose mind is preoccupied with
this world and its concerns, offers supplications without truly
understanding their essence. The deeds of an ascetic, however
small in quantity they maybe, are always better and more
valuable than those of a hedonist, however great in quantity
they maybe.

*Good works are the fruits of good circumstances; and
good circumstances are achieved through access to the
realms of spiritual realisation.*

As Imam Ghazālī said good knowledge is the source
of a good situation and a good situation is the source of
good deeds. Those who have access to the realms of spiritual
realisation (spiritual revelation) will enjoy good circumstances
in life. These good circumstances will always make them
perform good actions.

Allah's remembrance

Do not give up Allah's remembrance (dhikr) even though your mind is not in harmony with Allah. Forgetting His remembrance is worse than forgetting during His remembrance. Maybe, He will promote you from absent-minded remembrance to vigilant remembrance and from vigilant remembrance to remembrance with presence of Allah and from remembrance with presence of Allah to remembrance with the absence of everything except the Remembered. That is not difficult for Allah. (Qur'an, 14:20).

Here the author refers to various stages in the evolution of an initiate through Allah's remembrance. He is asked to remain in His remembrance even though he cannot always feel the presence of Allah, because absent-minded remembrance is better than none at all. Though his mind is not remembering Allah, his tongue is engaged in His remembrance. Later, he will be promoted from absent-minded remembrance to the next stage—vigilant remembrance, wherein does remembrance and contemplates Him in the mind at once. In the third stage, he can do remembrance and feel His presence simultaneously. And in the final stage, he will remember Allah' name with such a sublime mind that nothing except Allah will be present there at that time.

6

Death of the heart

If you neither feel regret about the opportunities of obedience you lost nor feel remorse for the mistakes you committed, it signifies the demise of your heart.

If the heart is alive with faith, it will regret the mistakes it has committed and feel remorse for the opportunities of obedience it has missed. A heart which is oriented towards Allah will rejoice at its abstention from sins and opportunities of obedience it could make use of. As the Messenger of Allah (ṣ) said, "the faithful one is he who is pleased with his good deeds and is annoyed by his bad deeds." It means the faithful person is basically fond of good deeds and harbours a grudge against bad deeds.

Do not despair of Him

Let no sin generate such gravity in your mind that it deprives you of your good opinion about Allah. He who knows his Lord truly, belittles his sin in front of His generosity.

Even a small fault on his part will hurt the faithful and he will consider it a grave mistake. He will soon repent of his mistake and pray for Allah's forgiveness. This seriousness reflects a positive and constructive approach. But, after committing a sin, if he is overwhelmed by a deep sense of despair and hopelessness regarding Allah's mercy and generosity, it reflects his ignorance of Allah, who is the Most Merciful and Generous. One should not posit his sin above Allah's munificence.

None of your sins will be trivial in front of His justice, and none of your sins will be severe in front of His grace.

No action of the servant, whether it be a commission or omission, will be significant if it's truly judged using proper divine yardsticks. No sin will be minor if it's properly judged by Allah's justice, and no sin will be major if it is seen through the spectacle of His generosity.

Deeds which you are not aware of and which you consider trivial are more likely to be accepted (by Allah).

The faithful should be very cautious about self-importance. He should never hold his deeds in high esteem but rather consider his role in them unimportant. His role in his deed is not important because had it not been for Allah's blessings, he could not have done it.

Divine inspiration

He only brought you an inspiration so that you can approach Him.

One whose heart is not purified by divine inspiration will not be able to understand Allah. Allah sends spiritual inspiration to purify His servant's heart so that it will be in a position to approach Him.

He brought you an inspiration so as to save you from the grip of vicissitudes and from the bondage of worldly things.

A mind preoccupied with worldly concerns is desperately isolated from the divine realm. Only divine inspiration could salvage man's heart from the bondage of alterities and the vicissitudes of life so as to enable it to enter the divine realm.

He brought you an inspiration so as to liberate you from the prison of your existence to the space of contemplation.

Only divine inspiration can take man from his mundane existence to the realm of spiritual contemplation. As long as man is imprisoned in his mundane existence, he cannot relish the flavour of spiritual contemplation.

Divine light

(Divine) lights are the horsepower of hearts and innermost secrets.

Divine light serves as a horse which takes on its back man's heart and innermost secret to the presence of Allah. Without the power and support of divine light man's heart will be denied access to the divine realm.

Light is the army of the heart, while darkness is the army of the self. So when Allah wants to help His servant, He will extend to him the forces of light and will cut him off from the forces of darkness and vicissitudes.

There are two conflicting forces operating within man: forces of the heart and forces of the self. The former is the force of good and light, while the latter is the force of evil and darkness. In the case of a good and sincere servant, the forces of light will get Allah's support and help against their opponents in this ongoing battle. The battle will eventually go in favour of the force which gets Allah's help.

Light generates illumination, and insight generates wisdom. It is up to the heart to decide on progression or regression.

Each one of the inner lights, the intellect and the heart, has a decisive role to play at various stages in the activities of an individual. Light will help the individual to identify the secret meanings of deeds, such as the goodness inherent in obedience and the evil intrinsic in disobedience. The intellect will judge and decide which is right or wrong, while the heart will take the final decision.

Self-effacing

*Let your obedience please you not because it has
stemmed from your but because it has originated from
Allah to You. " Say, 'In the bounty of Allah and in His
mercy—in that let them rejoice': That is better than
the (wealth) they hoard"* (Qurʾan, 10:58).

There are two types of pleasure that an individual may
feel after each act of obedience. He will be happy to think that
Allah has blessed him by selecting him to do a good deed. This
pleasure is laudable because it inspires him to be more thankful
to Allah. The second type of pleasure which is not desirable
comes from a sense of self-importance. It will persuade the
individual to highlight his role in the act of obedience and
make him forget Allah. This pleasure is malicious and harmful
to the health of the soul.

*He prevents both those who are still journeying to
Him and those who have already reached Him from
seeing their deeds and witnessing their circumstances.
As to the former, it was because they could not by
sincere to Allah in their deeds whereas in the case of
the latter He made them absent from them through
contemplating Him.*

Allah helps both those who are voyaging to Him and
those who have already reached Him in their acts of obedience
to ignore and undervalue their individual roles, albeit in
two different ways. The former will be worried about the
sincerity in their deeds. They will be unsatisfied with their
deeds because they doubt that they were up to the mark. This
frustration will go on haunting their minds so that they will

not be in a position to highlight their individual roles in their acts. On the other hand, the latter will be fully preoccupied with Allah, so that they will not get enough time to think about their personal acts. Lost in contemplation, as they are, how can they exult in what they did or did not?

7

Ambitions and delusions

*Had it not been for the seeds of ambition, the boughs
of disgrace could not have grown that lofty.*

Ambition is the root of all disgraces. People who are
fiercely ambitious will not hesitate to do any reprehensible
thing to achieve their worldly goals.

Nothing has misled you as your delusions.

Man is misled by suspicions and delusions. His misconception about himself, his life and its objectives have deviated
him from his stated goals. Delusions breed misconception and
unnecessary apprehensions in his mind and make him wash
his hands of all his responsibilities and live in a cloud-cuckoo-
land away from the realities of life.

*You are free from what you have despaired of, while
you are slave to what you crave for.*

Man is always a prisoner of his ambitions. He is free from
what he no longer wishes for and is a slave to what he is still

in pursuit of. Things he longs for will preoccupy his mind and hold him a prisoner till he achieves them. But things he has despaired of will no longer keep track of him.

Drawn to Him through misfortunes

Those who are not drawn to Allah through His affectionate caress will be led to Him shackled with adversities.

Some people will be drawn to Allah by His caress of love. They will identify Allah with His bounties. The more generous and munificent Allah becomes to them, the closer they will move to Him.

On the other hand, some people could not identify Allah even with the abundance of bounties He conferred on them. So Allah will drag them to Him with chains of misfortunes around their arms and legs. They may face adversities all through their lives because Allah knows that they would be distracted from Him if they were allowed to live different lives. In fact such lives are a blessing in disguise for them.

He who is not grateful for the graces (of Allah) runs the risk of losing them, while he who is grateful for them fastens them with their own ropes.

Those who are not thanking Allah for His graces may lose them at any time. They don't thank Allah because they are not afraid of losing them, even though they don't have any guarantee that Allah will continue to confer His bounties on them in the future also.

But those who thank Allah are trying their best to avoid an abrupt cessation of these divine graces. They thank Allah as

if they are fettering the graces with a rope so that they will not
run away.

Be on good terms with Him

Beware of His bounties offered to you while you are
still on bad terms with Him, gradually leading you
to a nemesis. "Those who reject Our signs, We shall
gradually visit with punishment, in ways they perceive
not" (Qur'an, 7:182).

Some people will be enjoying the generosity of Allah in
abundance although they are not on good terms with Allah.
But they do not know Allah is gradually taking them to
ruin and eternal failure. Allah is making them exult in their
temporary happiness while they are hardly bothered about the
nemeses awaiting them.

It's foolish for a novice to say, if the punishment
for his misdemeanour got delayed, that if it was a
misdemeanour, He would have cut off help and forced
isolation on him. Help could be taken away from him
in a way he does not understand, maybe through
denying further increase in it. And he could be kept
isolated in a way he does not know, maybe through
being given freedom to do what he pleases.

If the punishment for an improper conduct got delayed,
it does not mean Allah has no problem with your impropriety.
Allah must have started punishing you in a way that you do
not know or in a manner that you can hardly imagine. Maybe,

Allah has freed you from His control so that you will be doing whatever you please thereby walking unwittingly to the disaster awaiting you.

If you see a servant whom Allah has made remain reciting the litanies and extended His help therein, do not disregard what his Lord has bestowed on him because you could not notice in him signs of gnostics (enlightened servants) or the delight of lovers. For had it not been for an inspiration, there would have been no litany.

If you cannot perceive signs of gnostics in a person, it does not mean he is devoid of divine inspiration. If he recites litanies, it means he is still getting divine inspiration. You cannot underestimate him only because you are unable to see signs of gnostics in him. You are not entitled to guess as to his greatness on the basis of your criteria, and you are not an infallible judge on matters like this.

Service and love

Allah selects some people for His service and He reserves some others for loving Him. "Of the bounties of your Lord, We bestow freely on all—these as well as those: The bounties of your Lord are not closed (to anyone)" (Qur'an, 17:20).

Allah selects some of His servants for service and some others for love. If you are unable to distinguish those who are selected for service from those who are selected for love, how can you judge their greatness and decide their ranks? Only Allah can know the greatness and position of His servants.

⊠ ⊠ ⊠

8

Inspiration is not an achievement

It is rare that divine inspiration come suddenly except so that servants cannot claim that it comes by virtue of their preparations.

No one can claim that he receives divine inspiration because of his merits and hard work. Such a claim will allow him to attach unnecessary importance to his acts. Divine inspiration is not something that servants can achieve with their efforts only. It is Allah's grace and not the qualities and preparations of the servant that enabled him to receive divine inspiration.

The wise person knows his limit

If you see someone answering whatever he is asked, speaking of whatever he witnesses and talking about whatever he knows, it betokens his ignorance.

One who pretends to know everything and tries to answer to whatever one is asked is not a wise man at all. A wise man will be aware of the limitation of his knowledge and cautious about what he says. He will never show off his knowledge and experience and will not consider all his experiences and feelings worth sharing with people. A wise man is not one who produces answers to all questions he is asked, speaks about everything he witnesses and talks about everything he knows.

Eternal reward

> *He chose the hereafter as a place to reward His believing servants because this world is not wide enough to contain what He wants to confer on them and because He deemed their status too great to be rewarded in a world which is not eternal.*

Since this world is so transient and small, Allah has arranged another exclusive world, eternal and wide, for rewarding His obedient servants. The faithful person should not expect the reward for his deeds in this world, because he knows that this world is not the appropriate place for reward and punishment.

> *If one gets the fruits of one's deeds shortly (in this world), it is a confirmation of their acceptance in the long run (hereafter).*

In this world, an obedient servant will have a small glimpse of what he will be getting hereafter. As an acknowledgement of his obedience, Allah will give him in this world a small portion of the rewards awaiting him in the hereafter.

Situation indicates position

> *If you want to know your status with Him, take a look at where He made you stay.*

A servant who understands his situation in this world can also understand his position and status with Allah. Allah will facilitate more opportunities to know and worship Him for those who are really on good terms with Him. Those who are close to Allah can relish the sweetness of that closeness throughout their life.

Inward and outward blessings

Whenever He bestows on you obedience, making you not concerned about it because of Him, then feel sure that He has conferred on you His blessings both outwardly and inwardly.

One becomes an obedient servant if one is blessed by Allah outwardly, and one's mind becomes fully preoccupied with Allah if one is blessed by Allah inwardly. If Allah made you obedient and you became unaware of it because of your preoccupation with Allah, it means you are blessed both outwardly and inwardly by Allah.

9

Real pleading

The best you can solicit from Him is what He seeks from you.

The best thing for a servant to seek from His Lord is what He wants from him. If the servant asks what Allah wants from him, there will be no incongruity between the interest of the servant and the Lord, so that their relationship will be more harmonious.

Moreover, Allah knows better than anyone else what is better for His servant. What Allah seeks and expects from His servant will be better than anything the latter seeks for himself because Allah knows both the present and the past. He who created him in perfect symmetry and form and raised him when he was hardly able to do anything knows best what is good for him.

Real repentance

It is a travesty of penitence to regret the loss of opportunities of obedience without attempting to salvage the situation.

Repentance without efforts to rectify the errors is of no use. True repentance should be accompanied by a strong resolution and sincere efforts to correct the mistakes. Repentance without action is a weak sentiment that cannot bring about any tangible change.

The real signifier

A true gnostic (the enlightened servant) is not the one who, when he alludes (to one of the secrets of Allah), finds Allah closer to him than the allusion. But a gnostic is the one who has no allusion at all because of his extinction in His being and his absorption in contemplating Him.

One who reaches Allah by means of symbolic allusions needs some external signifiers to understand Allah. A true gnostic needs no symbolic allusions to understand Allah. He becomes united with Allah through self extinction. In his contemplation, he becomes so absorbed in Allah that nothing can divert his concentration. He knows that Allah is independent of anything and it is absurd to attribute Allah's existence to any signifier.

Real hope

Hope is supposed to be accompanied by deeds. Otherwise, it will become mere desire.

Hope unaccompanied by corresponding actions is a mere fancy that will not produce any change. No one can fulfil his dreams without taking practical steps towards it.

Real aspiration

The things a gnostic seeks from Allah are genuineness in servanthood and (the ability) to carry out privileges of the lordship.

What a gnostic always seeks from Allah is His blessings to be a sincere servant and to abide by the privileges of His lordship. The gnostic has no other personal ambition or aspiration other than proving himself a sincere servant. Since all his thoughts and prayers are preoccupied with this intense longing, he does not have anything else to ask of His Lord.

Real expansion

He spread you out so that you will not be remained contracted; and He contracted you so that you will not be left expanded. Then He removed you from both so that you will cease to belong to anything except Him.

Contraction (*al-qabḍ*) and expansion (*al-basṭ*) are the two initial stages for a spiritual initiate. Contraction is the first stage in which the spiritual aspirant abstains from all worldly attraction so that he can concentrate on worshiping and committing himself to Allah. In the second stage of expansion, the initiate will get access to all worldly things. This access makes him discern the triviality and temporariness of all material gains and the supremacy and eternity of the Creator. Only those with a strong determination and abiding steadfastness to ignore the attraction of this world can survive in the second stage. After emerging triumphant in this difficult stage, the gnostic will be able to enter the third and most important stage, where he goes above both contraction and expansion and understands Allah without any intermediary.

Gnostics are more afraid of being expanded than of being contracted, because, while expanded, only a few can stay within the limit of propriety.

The second stage, the stage of expansion, is very difficult because it involves a lot of trials that only the strong-minded can overcome with flying colours. The gnostics are very much cautious about this stage because they know well the hidden traps in it.

While expanded, the self will get its share through happiness; but while contracted, there is no share for the self.

In the stage of expansion the self is entitled to enjoy everything. It has no limitation at all, so that it will become very difficult for the individual to contain the self and constrain himself within the borders of propriety. In the stage of contraction, the self enjoys only a limited freedom so that there is not much to worry about.

The real gift

Sometimes He gives you (material gains) by depriving you (of closeness to Him), and sometimes He will deprive you (of material gains) by giving you (closeness to Him)

Sometimes, Allah may allot His servants the material riches while denying them closeness to Him. But no material gain can be a substitute for enjoying closeness to Allah. Being deprived of material riches is not a matter of concern for a true servant if he finds solace in being close to Allah. He considers this deprivation far better than being isolated from Allah. He is ready to cope with any deprivation if it helps him come closer to Allah. On the other hand, he hates any material gain that comes at the risk of alienating and separating him from Allah. He knows well that being close to Allah is far better than enjoying the material gains in complete isolation from Allah.

If He opens for you the door of cognisance while being deprived, the deprivation turns out to be a gift.

A true servant can turn any adversity in his life into a good opportunity to strengthen his relationship with Allah. He is capable of considering the deprivation a great opportunity to celebrate his submissiveness and glorify the magnificence and supremacy of His Lord. No deprivation, however challenging it maybe, can weaken him, as he is able to make a virtue of necessity. He considers any seemingly adverse situation a gift from the Almighty to admit his submissiveness and closeness to Him.

The real universe

The whole universe is an illusion in its outward manifestations, while inwardly it is an admonition. The self is fascinated by its illusive exterior, while the heart is drawn by its admonitory interior.

The universe is a two-pronged weapon which is too dangerous to handle. One must be very careful and cautious about using it. One should not allow oneself to be drawn by the veneer of its glitz without seeing the traps inherent in it. Its outward appearance is so illusory and deceptive as to distract man from seeing its innate admonition. The self is prone to being easily cheated by superficialities, while only an insightful mind can go beyond the illusive exterior and identify the traps.

Real glory

If you are seeking eternal glory, do not revel in a glory that will not last.

The universe is not worth trusting. For one who seeks eternal glory, this transient world is not the place to do so. If there is nothing enduring in this world, why should one waste one's time and energy in pursuing its glories?

The real journey

The real journey is to cross the precincts of this world in order that the hereafter will become closer to you than yourself.

Nothing in this world will be the final destination of one who is seriously aware of its limitation and temporariness. He considers the border of this world the place to start the real journey from. The hereafter is the final destination of the faithful.

Real deprivation

A gift from creatures is (really) deprivation, while deprivation from Allah is (really) munificence.

As no gift from creatures has an enduring value, whatever it brings will not be compared to gifts from Allah. Even deprivation, if it is from Allah, is far better than any valuable gift from a creature.

⚅ ⚅ ⚅

10

Reward

Far be it from our Lord to reward the servant with credit while he deals with Him in cash.

When a devoted servant offers worship to Allah in this world, Allah is not so ungenerous as to postpone the reward to a later occasion—the hereafter. He will make the servant savour in this world the flavour of the reward awaiting him in the hereafter.

His recognising you as worthy of obedience will suffice as a reward for your obedience.

The great reward an obedient servant deserves in this world is the light of faith and piety. He became obedient because Allah found him worthy of obedience. It means Allah has selected him for obedience and made him a distinguished servant. Had it not been for Allah's blessings, he would not have had an opportunity to understand and worship Allah. If Allah gives you an opportunity to live as an obedient servant, it suggests that you are getting the most important reward for your obedience. One who is denied an opportunity to

understand and worship Allah is leading the most tragic and
ill-fated life, whatever material riches and fame he may enjoy.

❖

*It will suffice as a reward for servants (those who do
good deeds) to have something that inspires their
hearts to obedience and brings to them amusement.*

One who finds entertainment and pleasure in one's
worships can feel sure that one is being fittingly rewarded for
obedience. It means he belongs to the distinguished people
whose hearts are thrilled at the prospect of worshipping Allah.
Only those who are blessed by Allah can find enjoyment
in being obedient to Allah. They need no other means of
entertainment in this world, as worshiping Allah is the most
favourite entertainment and hobby for them. They can make
their lives more enjoyable and meaningful through their
closeness to Allah. They do not consider obligatory prayers
a burden but rather a means of pleasure and amusement
to relieve the boredom of material life, which is full of
meaningless glitz and glamour.

❖

*Those who worship Him, aspiring something from
Him or to fend off an impending chastisement, do not
attach to His attributes their due value.*

For a true servant, worshiping Allah must be both the
means and end. It is not a means to achieve something in
return or to stave off any punishment or trial. If the worshiper
has another objective, it affects his sincerity.

❖

Deprivation as a blessing

*When He gives, He makes you witness His
benevolence, and when He denies you (something),
He makes you witness His supremacy. And in both
situations, He is making Himself discernible to you
and approaching you with His gentleness.*

Allah shows His kindness to His servants by bestowing
His bounties on them, while He shows His supremacy to
them by depriving them of fortunes in life. In both cases, He is
making Himself known to them. Both prosperity and adversity
come from Allah. A true servant considers them two different
means to know and understand Allah. He has no difficulty
in coping with any seemingly adverse situation in life, as he
deems it an opportunity to understand Allah in a different
way.

*Deprivation hurts you because you fail to understand
Allah in it.*

Only those who could not understand Allah truly will fail
to understand the true meaning of an adverse situation. No
adverse situation will be painful for one who understands its
intrinsic meaning and the divine purpose behind it.

*Sometimes He opens the door of obedience for you but
without opening the door of acceptance; or sometimes
He will condemn you to sin which may turn out to be
a cause of reaching Him.*

All deeds of a seemingly obedient servant may not be
accepted by Allah. That one is obedient does not mean one's

acts are so immaculate as to be acknowledged and accepted
by Allah. One who worships just to show off or to win any
material advantage will not be able to earn Allah's approval. In
such cases, he is unable to reach Allah despite his worship.

On the contrary, a sinner must not necessarily end up a
sinner. He maybe going through a temporary period of trial
ahead of his repentance and redemption. Maybe, he will be
enlightened on Allah while revelling in his sins. Allah may give
the sinner an opportunity to experience His presence through
repentance and tears.

*A sin that leads to humiliation and neediness is better
than obedience that leads to pride and arrogance.*

The true purpose behind obedience is the submissiveness
of the servant in front of Allah. The natural motivations
behind the sin are arrogance and defiance because only those
who dare defy and challenge Allah's decrees can deliberately
commit a sin. But if the obedience does not serve its real
purposes such as submissiveness and humbleness, but tends to
produce the opposite traits, the line of demarcation between
obedience and sin will be blurred.

One who is routinely worshipping Allah may grow
complacent about one's position and status, while a sinner
may one day turn remorseful for what he has done and, in so
doing, will be persuaded to mend his relationship with Allah.
The sinner may possibly feel regret and weep bitter tears of
repentance in front of Allah, admitting his submissiveness and
humbleness. Therefore the sin that eventually leads to remorse
and compunction is better than obedience that engenders only
self-infatuation and arrogance.

Two divine bounties that no being can be separated from and are unavoidable for every creature are existence and sustenance.

Existence and sustenance are the two divine graces with which Allah blessed all His creatures.

He conferred on you, initially, the grace of existence, which was followed by the grace of sustenance.

Allah created man from nothingness and gave him whatever he requires to live in this world. He would have been nothing had Allah not created him; and he would have been incapable of doing anything had Allah not conferred on him His blessings. Man's existence itself demands his servitude to Allah because he is indebted to Him for his existence. This servitude should exist till his death because he is indebted to Allah for his sustenance till the end of his life.

So your destitution essentially belongs to you. The trials in this world are but reminders of the aspects of your destitution that are hidden from you. No emergency can alter the essential destitution.

Essentially, man does not own anything, as he is born and dies destitute. When he was born he was not able to do anything on his own, and when he dies he leaves behind whatever he earned. Whatever he has achieved or claimed to have achieved is owned by Allah. When he is confronted with any difficulty in life, he cannot complain of any injustice or unfair treatment because whatever he lost was not really his rights. On the contrary, the trials and tribulations of life should remind him of his essential destitution and help him bring to mind his real picture. If man is essentially destitute, no temporary achievements in this transient life can alter his essential state.

The best of your moments are those wherein you witness the existence of your destitution and thereby the existence of your submissiveness.

The best thing demanded of man is his admission of servitude. He feels his servitude and submissiveness to Allah when he experiences his destitution. Poverty that makes one contemplate Allah is better than the riches that make one oblivious of Allah.

When He isolates you from His creatures, it means He wants to open for you the door of amusement with Him.

If worldly associations and contacts prevent one from establishing and maintaining a relationship with Allah, he should keep himself away from such contacts.

Isolation from the material world, if it is advised and imposed by Allah, is better than seeking the companionship of what takes him away from Allah.

When He makes you utter a request, it means He wants to give you something.

Allah knows best what is good for His servant, so that He makes him long and pray for that. Even the prayer for a good thing does not stem from the servant's intention but springs from his Lord's persuasions.

Needs will never desert the gnostic. And he will anchor himself only to Allah.

Nothing can satiate a gnostic who could not find comfort in anything but Allah.

He wants to always be in need of Allah and enjoys the state of being in need of His grace. He does not want anyone else but Allah. He turns down all offers from creatures but enjoys begging of Allah.

He illuminated the exteriors with the light of His creatures; and He illuminated the interiors (innermost hearts) with the light of His attributes. Therefore, when the light of the exteriors set, the light of the interiors and innermost hearts will not set. That is why it is said: "Verily, the sun of the day sets in the night; but the sun of the heart will never set."

The glittering glamour of this world will never vanquish the heart of a gnostic, which is illuminated with the eternal divine light. Allah illuminates the heart of His beloved servant with His attributes, so that nothing can extinguish it at any time. How can the ephemeral outshine the eternal? But He illuminates the external world with the light of His creatures which is ephemeral and can be turned off at any time. The light of this world will set anytime, while the divine light will remain forever.

11

Everything is from Him

*In order to assuage the sufferings of tribulations, He
has taught you that it is He who tests you. The One
who made you confront His predestination is the same
one who has accustomed you to good choices.*

A believer finds solace in the remembrance of Allah. The
thought that everything comes from Allah is an inspiration
for the faithful throughout his life. He will not be bemused
by anything that happens in his life because he has trust in
Allah, who is the Creator and Destroyer of everything. The
realisation that he is being tested by none other than his
Cherisher and Creator encourages him to enjoy the situation
with submissiveness and dedication. He considers any adverse
situation in life an opportunity to display his true dedication
and commitment to Allah and to understand his Lord from a
different angle. The realisation that it is Allah who brings forth
both adversity and prosperity in his life makes him face the
situation without showing any grudge. How dare he question
or dislike anything from Allah?

*Those who imagine that His kindness is detached from
His predestination does so out of short-sightedness.*

A comprehensive understanding of Allah includes understanding all His attributes without any discrimination. If one fails to understand any attribute of Allah, it betrays one's short-sightedness. One who understands Allah in His wholeness cannot differentiate His kindness from His predestination. One who relishes the graces of Allah should not grudge having to suffer His trials also.

Beware of passions

*Do not fear that the way (to Allah) maybe puzzling to
you; but feel afraid of passion overpowering you.*

An initiate need not bother about the complications on his way to Allah. But he has to be cautious about his own passions, which may distract him from his goals and endanger his spiritual prospects. Passion poses more dangerous a threat to the spiritual health of the individual than anything else.

Duality

*Praise be to Him who has covered the exclusive
secrets with the exteriors of human nature and who
showed the sublimity of lordship through manifesting
servanthood (to the servants).*

Duality is inherent in human nature. His exclusive holiness coexists with his common human traits. A man who owns a mind illuminated with divine light may look like an ordinary human in his original form. His common human nature helps him hide his loftiness and exclusivity.

Blaming Yourself

Do not complain to your Lord about a delayed reply to your request; but you should rather complain about yourself for your delayed (misplaced) manners.

If there is a delay in getting Allah's reply for your request, there is no point in complaining about it, because the delay happened due to your own mistakes. How can you ignore all other delays on your part and bother about the delay from Allah? When you have procrastinated and delayed in your duties towards your Lord, you were least bothered about the problems that ensued. But now that you are not getting a reply for your request when you want to get it, you have soon become aware of the problems of delaying. So, before lodging a complaint against the delay, you have to rectify the mistakes and delays on your part.

Obedience is a great gift

Whenever He makes you obedient to His command openly and makes you acknowledge His power in secret, it means He has bestowed on you a great favour.

The most blessed servant is the one who obeys Allah, acknowledging His greatness and magnificence. If one could worship Allah openly and admit His power in secret, it means one has received from Allah one of the greatest blessings.

Consistency

Not all those whose exclusiveness was confirmed could perfect their liberation.

The real exclusiveness or distinction of a servant is his consistency in obedience (*istiqāmah*). Any exclusiveness devoid of this consistency is imperfect and vulnerable to degeneration at any time. If a servant claims distinction in the sense that he can perform miracles or extraordinary things, it does not mean he is perfect in terms of consistency. The exclusiveness of those who attained consistency in obedience is superior to that of those who perform miracles. Therefore the latter have gone only halfway towards achieving their end, while the former have perfected their immunity from all sorts of threats to spiritual integrity.

12

Litanies

Only the ignorant ones could underestimate the litany (wird). While the litany will disappear along with this world, the inspiration drawn from it (wārid) will be intact till the hereafter. It is advisable to engage in something for which there is no alternative. The litany is what He seeks from you, while the inspiration is what you seek from Him. But where is what He asks from you compared to what you seek from Him?

In the broadest sense of the word, *litany* encompasses a wide spectrum of supplications and good deeds which help a servant illuminate his mind with divine inspiration. An initiate cannot underestimate the significance of the litany because it is a prerequisite to get the inspiration. The former is the duty of the servant, while the latter is his right from Allah. He has to carry out his duties diligently before staking claim for his rights. Moreover, as a servant he has to be very careful to utilise his time and energy to carry out his duties. He cannot seek whatever he wishes from Allah before making himself acceptable to Allah through constant dedication and supplication. He is asked to concentrate on his duties rather than bothering about what there is to come from Allah.

Eligibility

The arrival of sustenance (from Allah) depends on the preparations (of the servant), while the dawning of light is in accordance with innermost purity.

The servant's preparedness to obey Allah is an important factor in getting spiritual sustenance from Allah; and his heart's purity is a prerequisite for getting Allah's help. He has to do everything in his capacity to deserve Allah's support and sustenance for his enterprise. Only those who have fixed themselves on the course of Allah with true dedication and actions can expect His provisions for his journey. And only a purified mind can be a fitting reservoir of divine light. An irresolute and irresponsible person and an impure mind are not eligible candidates for spiritual enlightenment. Only those who tend to utilise the faculties given by Allah can expect additional supplies from Him.

From creature to Creator

An ignorant man gets up thinking about what he is going to do, while an intelligent man reflects on what Allah is doing with him.

Somene who is too preoccupied with his deeds to think about Allah is truly ignorant because he is concerned only with the things inside the narrow precincts of his life and is not aware of what is going on outside. An intelligent man pays little heed to his acts because he knows their triviality and temporariness compared to Allah's deeds and strategies.

Both devotees and ascetics seek to distance themselves from everything because for them Allah is absent from everything. If they witnessed Allah in everything, they would not have sought detachment from anything.

Devotees and ascetics seek alienation from everything other than Allah because they cannot find His presence in anything else. All creatures are essentially dependent, imperfect and defective in one way or another. They cannot possess even a single attribute of Allah. But for devotees and ascetics Allah is the only destination. No creature satisfies them because anything that falls short of Allah cannot content them. They want Allah and only Allah. When they came to know that nothing in this world can satisfy their objectives, they opted for isolation and alienation.

He asked you in this world to reflect on His creatures; but in the hereafter, He will reveal to you His perfect entity.

In this world, Creation is the most perceptible, ubiquitous and active divine phenomenon. Therefore man is asked to explore the wonders of Creation to delve deep into the realms of divine secrets. The more profoundly one understands the diversity and beauty of Creation, the more broadly one can understand the Creator. But no one can expect to see Allah's perfect entity in this world. It will be revealed to him only in the hereafter. While Allah can be understood through His creation in this world, He will be revealed with His perfect entity only in the hereafter.

Concessions

Since He knows that you could not endure without (seeing) Him, He made you see what is perceptible from Him (His creatures).

Allah has made Himself imperceptible to His creatures in this world; but He made Himself known through His creatures. Since Allah knew that His servants would not bear not being able to see Him in this world, He reflected His presence in His creatures.

Since Allah knows that you would be exhausted, He conferred on you different means of obedience. And since Allah knew your impulsiveness, He restricted it to certain times so that you will be concerned more with performing devotional prayers than with the existence of the prayer itself. For not all those who pray perform it (well).

Man was created for worshipping Allah. The gnostic will never be tired of worshipping Allah nor will he complain about boredom. But Allah, who knows His servant's weaknesses and whims and fancies better than anyone else, has created diverse forms of worship and a schedule and system for them lest it may appear to him too monotonous and exhausting. Considering man's convenience, Allah introduced diversity and a systematic schedule for devotional prayers as an encouragement to bring forth better results. The timing of the prayers helps the servant concentrate on performing the prayers rather than worrying about their existence. Allah has restricted them to certain times, leaving the responsibility of performing them better up to the servant.

Compulsory prayers

Devotional prayers purify hearts from dirt and open up the door to the domain of secrets.

Devotional prayers (prayers offered five times a day) are a means arranged by Allah to purify the heart of the servant and train it to prepare for accepting divine inspiration. One cannot ignore the bigger role of devotional prayers in getting access to the spiritual domains.

Devotional prayers are the place of conversation (between the servant and his Lord) and reciprocal gestures wherein the domains of the secrets will be widened and the gleams of light will crack open. He knows your weakness, so that He reduced the number of devotional prayers. And He knows that you want His grace, so that He multiplied their productivity.

Devotional prayers are an opportunity for the servant to communicate with His Lord. The servant is asked to be very vigilant, conscious and pious while offering his prayer. As the Messenger of Allah (ṣ) succinctly said to the archangel Jibrīl, who appeared in front of him disguised as a student, "Worship Him as if you see Him. Even if you do not see Him, He sees you." The prayer is an opportunity for the servant to liberate himself from his pretty mundane existence to the gleaming divine spheres, where he will enjoy conversing with His Lord and basking in the divine light. But Allah knows that man is not always able to enjoy such a communication with His Lord. Therefore He restricted the prayers to five times a day and increased their reward also.

No right to ask for reward

When you seek reward in exchange for a deed, you will be questioned about the sincerity in it. For the insincere, safety from chastisement will be enough (as a reward).

Prayers devoid of sincerity and commitment are not worthy of consideration. If it is not spiced up with sincerity and commitment, the prayer becomes a vain and spiritless exercise. There is a great difference between worshipping Allah for Allah and worshipping Allah for oneself. If a servant worships Allah for achieving any personal purpose, such as reward or exclusion from chastisement, it betrays his insincerity. He is not entitled to get any reward from Allah, because saving him from chastisement itself will be enough for him as reward.

Do not seek reward for a deed which you did not actually do. That He accepts it will be enough as reward for you.

Had it not been for Allah's help, man would have been totally incapable of doing anything. If Allah were the actual doer of our deeds, our claim for reward would be uncalled for. If we considered our role in our deeds trivial, we would be ashamed of asking Allah for rewards. His acceptance itself is a great reward.

✦

When He wants to reveal His grace to you, He creates (good) deeds (in you) and attributes them to you.

Allah helps His good servant to do good deeds, facilitating all necessary arrangements for it. He creates a favourable situation and context for it so that the servant can perform the deeds without any difficulty. For a servant this blessing is the most important grace from Allah. Allah selects only His good servants to worship Him and protects them from committing mistakes.

✦

If He made you resort to yourself, there will be no end to your desolation; and if He confers His munificence on you, there will be no end to your fortunes.

Nothing can save you from the isolation and deprivation imposed by Allah, and nothing can prevent you from His munificence. Without Allah's blessings, all your efforts will go in vain. If you are deprived of divine help, nothing can help you; and if you are getting Allah' support and blessings, no hurdle will be insurmountable for you.

✦ ✦ ✦

13

Human attributes versus divine attributes

*Associate yourself with the attributes of His Lord-
ship to make you aware about attributes of your
servanthood.*

To understand Allah thoroughly one has to understand
His every attribute. This will enable him to compare and
contrast his lowliness and Allah's magnificence, his inferiority
and Allah's superiority, his deprivation and Allah's prosperity,
his dependence and Allah's independence, his transience and
Allah's eternity, his obedience and Allah's supremacy and
finally his servanthood and Allah's Lordship. Only through
observing Allah's attributes and reflecting on their features can
one understand Allah's greatness and his lowliness.

*He has forbidden you from laying claim to what does
not belong to you from the attributes of His creatures,
let alone laying claim to attributes of Him who is the
Lord of the universe.*

Man is allowed to use and enjoy whatever is given to
him. But he is not entitled to claim the qualities, attributes

and belongings of someone else, the worst being his claim to something that is exclusive to Allah. Claiming Allah's attributes amounts to a blatant violation of his limitations as a servant. It is a grave sin because he is seeking in vain to juxtapose Allah's eternal attributes with his transient self.

How can extraordinary things happen to you, when you have yet to rip apart the ordinariness of your life?

Man, who cannot transcend the ordinariness of his life, cannot expect something extraordinary in his life. Only those who have succeeded in vanquishing their worldly ambitions and passions and developed themselves to an extraordinary realm deserve to do extra ordinary things. How can one who is desperately stuck in the ordinariness of his life perform extraordinary things for others?

It is not important that you beg (Allah) but the important thing is whether you conform to good conduct or not.

Conforming to the etiquettes of servanthood is more important for the servant than begging Allah. He has to maintain a sense of decorum demanded of him before asking Allah. Those who do not observe the virtuous conduct prescribed by Allah are violating a crucial prerequisite for begging Allah.

Nothing is so demanded of you as extreme need; and nothing so expedites gifts as lowliness and need.

Extreme need of Allah is what the servant wants the most. He should believe that he cannot do anything without Allah's help. He should imagine himself totally helpless and extremely in need of Allah's support, as if he were clutching at straws to escape from danger. Displaying one's lowliness and need in front of Allah is a means to get an immediate reply from Him.

If you do not hope to reach Him without the extinction of your defects and the effacement of your self-importance, you will never reach Him. When He wants you to reach Him, He will hide your attributes with His attributes and your qualities with His qualities. Thus, He makes you reach Him by virtue of what comes from Him and not by means of what comes from you to Him.

Defects and pretentions are some basic and indivisible human attributes. If the servant thinks he can reach Allah by eliminating his vices and pretensions through his hard work, he will never reach Allah. To reach Allah is an exclusive gift from Allah and it will not be acquired through the efforts of the servant. On the other hand, if Allah wants a servant to reach Him, He will hide his attributes and qualities with His attributes and qualities. A servant is not able to reach Allah with his own efforts but He wants action on Allah's part to this effect. It means his efforts, however sincere they maybe, are not capable of taking him to Allah without Allah's help and support.

14

The veneer

Had it not been for His beautiful veneer (of protection),
no deed would be worthy of acceptance.

The servant cannot claim that his obedience will be
accepted by Allah. His prayers and supplications will not be
faultless and there will always be some room for improvement.
If Allah, the Merciful, does not forgive him, covering his
defects with His kindness, none of his prayers will be worthy of
acceptance.

You need His forbearance more when you obey Him
than when you disobey Him.

An obedient servant is more in need of Allah's magnanimity
than a disobedient servant. The former needs Allah to forgive
his defects, to accept his obedience and to help him retain and
improve his present situation. He is also obliged to praise Allah
for blessing him with the opportunity to worship Him, which a
number of others have been denied.

There are two types of veneer (protection): one that protects you from disobedience and one that protects you in disobedience. The layman who is afraid of losing his status among people seeks Allah's covering in disobedience, while the privileged one who is afraid of losing his position with the Real King seeks Allah's protection from disobedience.

The gnostic seeks Allah's covering from the sin, while the layman wants Allah's covering for his sins. The gnostic who always bothers about preserving his status and image with Allah seeks Allah's covering to protect him from any thing that will affect his position with Allah. He is more concerned about his image being tarnished in front of Allah than in front of people. On the other hand, an ordinary man who is always concerned about his status and image among people seeks Allah's covering for his disobedience so that nobody will see his sins. When the former seeks from Allah His protection, the latter seeks from Allah protection from creatures.

Those who hold you in high esteem honour the beauty of your veneer. Therefore, praise the One who veneered you and not the one who honoured and thanked you.

When people admire you they are admiring your superficial beauty, because Allah has protected you with a veil so that they cannot see your vulgarities. Whenever people are honouring you, they are honouring the veneer and not the core. Therefore, you are obliged to praise the one who veiled your vulgarities and not the one who respected you without being able to see your vulgarities.

The real companion is the one who accompanies you despite his knowing your defects. This (companion) is none other than your Lord. The best companion is the one who chooses you without expecting any benefit from you in return.

Allah protects His servant better than anyone even though He knows his defects better than anyone. He has bestowed on him His graces without desiring anything in return.

Towards certitude

When the light of certitude dawns on you, you will see the hereafter so close that you need not travel towards it, and you will see the splendours of this world exposed to the eclipse of extinction.

When a believer gradually reaches the level of absolute certitude, no doubt will remain in his mind about the imminent end of this world and the arrival of an enduring world. This certitude will save him from all illusions about this world and its glitz, which is really meant to be destroyed. True knowledge serves to emancipate man from ignorance and suspicion about himself and the world he lives in.

It is not the existence of something else alongside Him that veils you from Him. But what veils you from Him is your illusion that something is there alongside Him.

There exists nothing to cover up Allah from servants, because Allah will be visible in everything that tries to hide Him. It is only because of his weakness and illusion that man is not able to perceive Allah.

Had it not been for His manifestation in creatures, (human) eyes would not have perceived them. If His attributes were manifested, creatures would have faded away.

Creatures are dependent on Allah for their existence and worth. Allah has made His presence felt in His creatures so that human eyes can perceive them. Without this divine touch, nothing would be worth perceiving. But creatures are not capable of bearing Allah's attributes. Divine attributes will be too heavy for them to carry. They are blessed with divine manifestation and not with divine attributes.

He made everything manifest because He is the Interior, and He obscured the existence of everything because He is the Exterior.

Allah is simultaneously the Interior and the Exterior, as He describes Himself in the noble Qur'an. Allah is the Interior compared to the exteriority of creature and He is the Exterior compared to the interiority of creatures. To put it differently, the world of creatures is so exterior and superficial that they do not have access to anything interior and profound. Their world is also so interior and narrower that they do not have access to the broader horizons of the divinity. Allah is the Interior because He knows well what lies in the deep. Allah is the Exterior also because He knows well what is in the air and on the heavens.

He allows you to reflect on creatures. But He does not allowed you to stay there with those creatures. With His words "Say, 'Behold all that is in the heavens and on earth!'" (Qur'an, 10:101), He opened up the door of understanding for you. But He does not say, "Behold the heavens," so as not to stop you at their corporal existence.

This world is not an end in itself. Man is asked to consider this universe and all the creatures in it as only a means to an end—Allah and the hereafter. Allah asks him to reflect on this world to understand its transience and the eternity of its Creator. Allah asks him to reflect on His creatures to understand Him well. Man should not allow himself to be distracted by the beauty of this world.

The universe became stable when He made it stable but it is effaced viewed through the unity of His being.

The stability of this universe is only illusory. It became stable when Allah made it stable. Although it appears to be permanent it is doomed to be dismantled at any time. All creatures are dependent on their Creator and at the mercy of His power. He is the Perpetual and Eternal, and everything other than Him is transient. The unity of His being demands their extinction at any time.

15

Ward off people's accolades

People praise you for what, according to their supposition, is yours; so you must blame yourself for what you know of those praises.

A true believer thinks too little of people's praises and admiration for his deeds, because he knows well he does not deserve any credit for them. He thinks that Allah is the real cause of everything and only He deserves praises from any source. He blames himself for people's admiration for him and wants to be away from it, as he considers himself an unworthy recipient.

When a believer is lauded, he feels ashamed in front of Allah of being praised for an attribute that he cannot perceive in himself.

A believer who is praised by people is really ashamed of himself when he confronts Allah, because he has got credit for something which he does not deserve at all. He feels guilty because he knows himself better than others do and he believes that he was erroneously given credit for what Allah has done.

❖

The most ignorant one is he who forgoes his certitude for people's suppositions.

One should not allow himself to be drawn by people's opinions about him. He knows himself better than people; and people's opinions about him stem from their suppositions and imaginations, while his opinion about himself comes from his certitude.

When he suspects his certitude about himself and Allah and accepts people's suppositions about him, he is doing injustice to his own conscience.

❖

When He makes people praise you for what you do not deserve, praise Him for what He deserves.

A believer cannot enjoy people's praising him, as he is disturbed by accepting what he does not deserve. In order to get rid of this distaste, he praises Allah, who deserves all praises and admiration for what he did.

❖

When ascetics are lauded, they are contracted because they perceive the praises hailing from creatures; but when gnostics are praised, they are expanded because they perceive it coming from the real King.

There is an obvious difference between how ascetics and gnostics consider praises and admiration from people. Ascetics (*zuhhād*) are averse to the praises of people, as they are afraid that it may adversely affect their relationship with Allah. They are expecting everything from Allah and nothing from people. So accepting anything from people, they fear, will affect what they are going to get from Allah. On the contrary, the gnostics, who are in a more elevated position and enjoys a closer relationship with Allah, are least concerned by what people think about them. They don't think that anything can weaken their strong relationship with Allah. They take a different stance to people's admiration and consider it to be coming from Allah. Whenever people praise them, it does not create any difficulty for them, as they consider it an opportunity to understand Allah more and more. For them, everything comes from Allah and nothing other than Allah is not in the picture.

If something given to you expands you and if something denied to you contracts you, it betokens your immaturity (or triviality because you are an uninvited guest among gnostics) and the insincerity of your servanthood.

One who is delighted when getting something and falls in despair when denied something is not a true gnostic. It is indicative of his insincerity because his opinion of Allah changes according to what he gets from Allah. But he is an uninvited guest or an immature one among gnostics.

16

Be optimistic about Him

*When you commit a sin, let it not make you despair
of being righteous with your Lord, because it might be
the last sin predestined for you.*

A true believer will not allow a mistake he commits to
weaken his determination and make him despair of Allah's
mercy; but he will take it an opportunity to improve his
relationship with Allah through repentance and supplication
and to compensate for his fault. He will admit his mistake and
take a new resolution not to commit the sin again.

*If you want the door of hope opened for you, bring to
mind whatever (bounties) He conferred on you. And
if you want the door of fear opened for you, bring to
mind whatever you did to Him.*

If remembering Allah's generosity is a means to be
more hopeful of Allah, the way to increase fear of Allah is to
compare notes with what Allah has given to one and what
one has given to Allah. A servant can increase his optimism
about the blessings of Allah by recalling all that He has done

for him. When he understands Allah's boundless mercy and generosity, it will increase his trust in Allah. Those who do not remember Allah's graces will soon despair of His generosity. If he recalls what he has given to Allah in return, it will make him understand his shortcomings and defects. It also makes him cautious of his deeds and generates in him fear of Allah.

Contraction and expansion

Sometimes He will teach you in the night of contraction what you have not learned in the bright day of expansion. "You know not which of them is nearest to you in benefit" (Qur'an, 4:11).

As mentioned earlier, gnostics prefer the state of contraction to that of expansion because the self has only a limited role in the former, while the self has been given a free rein in the latter. Here the night and day are employed as metaphors for contraction and expansion. A servant can understand within the constraints of contraction what he is not able to understand in the freedom of expansion. Therefore, Allah holds some of His servants in a state of contraction because He wants them to understand and experience what they may not do so if they were in a state of expansion.

Dawn of light

Hearts and innermost secrets are the places where lights dawn.

The heart of a gnostic is likened to the heavens illuminated by the stars of knowledge, the moon of wisdom and the sun of cognisance. Allah brightens His dear servant's heart with divine light, which outshines all other sources of material light. Even the light of the sun, moon and stars are dwarfed by the dazzling divine light that illumines the heart of a gnostic.

If the heart is cut off from divine light, it loses all its sheen and is no longer be powerful against darkness. Bereft of divine light, the heart loses much of its immunity against inner diseases.

The light deposited in hearts is nourished by the light issuing from invisible treasures—the light which unveils to you the states of His creatures and the light which unveils to you His attributes.

The light absorbed by the heart of a gnostic will always be nurtured by the lights emanating from divine realms. The radiance of his heart is really the radiance of divine light. Since no worldly light can outperform divine light, the heart which is being constantly furnished with divine light will be powerful against all forces of darkness.

Seen in this light, the insignificance of this world and the importance of the hereafter will become more visible for the viewer. This light will help him see the triviality and transience of all creatures and the magnificence and eternity of their Lord.

Sometimes hearts will be stopped along with the lights just as souls will be veiled by the opacity of vicissitudes.

The light itself is not the end but ought to be only a means to Allah. If the light turns out to be the end instead of a means, it means the heart has lost its momentum and stopped en route. When the servant concentrates on the light and its superficial glitter rather than focusing on his journey to Allah, he is desperately stuck halfway.

Surprisingly, the light which is supposed to be a guide obstructs the spiritual course just as the alterities and vicissitudes of life blur the transparency of the soul. In such a situation, there is basically no difference between light and alterity, with the former blocking the progress of the heart and the latter creating hurdles for the soul.

In order to honour the inner lights (lights of innermost secrets), He veiled them with opaque exteriors so that they will not be degraded by the exteriors or be accused of seeking fame.

Allah has honoured the inner light of the gnostic. So in order to protect it from all sorts of harms and degradation, He created an opaque exterior to hide it and to protect it from external threats. This exterior will help the gnostic keep his inner light away from people and their opinions. He does not exhibit it in front of people nor does he make any claim about it, so that he can preserve and maintain it appropriately.

17

Secrets of saints

Glorified be He who has not made any sign indicative
of His saints except for the signs indicative of Him,
and who has not led anyone to them except for the one
who He wanted to lead to Him.

Saints are Allah's chosen and hallowed servants. Allah
has elevated them to higher echelons and distinguished them
from others in many respects. But Allah has made the signs
leading to them so imperceptible for other servants that they
cannot identify a saint very easily. It is very difficult to identify
and recognise them because Allah has made their interiors
inaccessible to the common people, closing all doors and
ways to it. As we mentioned earlier, Allah has honoured their
secrets and covered their sainthood with their common nature
and appearance. Just as oysters seen on the mudflat hide
invaluable pearls inside them, Allah has hidden the beauty
of their sainthood with a rough covering that will not betray
what is inside.

Only the blessed ones who are selected by Allah to reach
Him can make it to the secrets of His saints. Even such a

dignified servant as prophet Moses could not easily decipher the secrets of a saint like Khaḍir, let alone an ordinary man.

Sometimes He discloses to you the invisibilities of His realm but prevents you from having a glimpse of the secrets of servants.

Sometimes, understanding saints will be more difficult than reaching Allah. This happens when Allah opens a crack to His secrets for the servant without letting him know the secrets of another servant. Understanding the saint is an exclusive right for a privileged few, while understanding and reaching Allah is allowed to more people. Only those who can deal with the secrets of saints appropriately will be allowed access to them.

He who happens to know the secrets of servants without accommodating himself to divine mercy finds his knowledge an ordeal and a precursor of the evils to come.

Knowledge about the secrets of the saints is a two-pronged weapon. If Allah has not blessed one with the ability to discern and discriminate the facts, this knowledge may itself turn out to be a great danger. All knowledge seeks some sorts of responsibility. The knowledge will be a burden for those who are not able to comply with such responsibilities. Ignorance which is not harmful is better than knowledge which is detrimental to spiritual growth.

One's share in obedience and disobedience

The body' share in disobedience is outward and apparent, while its share in obedience is inward and hidden. Treating what is hidden (of ailments) is very difficult.

The body will be apparently persuaded to commit a sin because it has an immediately obvious interest in it. The body is likely to be beguiled into committing a sin because it always seeks pleasure and satisfaction in disobedience. But it will not be that easily persuaded to obey Allah because it fails to find a means of enjoyment in obedience. Only those who can reflect on the hidden and implicit advantages of worshipping Allah can find solace and enjoyment in obedience. So it is very difficult to persuade the self to worship Allah while it is very easy to persuade it to commit a sin. A mind concerned about worldly gains and temporary advantages is more prone to be attracted to disobedience, while only a mind that seriously ruminates over what is better in the long run will be interested in obedience.

Explicit and implicit ostentations

Sometimes ostentation invades you in a place where nobody notices you.

There are two types of ostentations: explicit and implicit. In the explicit ostentation, the individual enjoys a secret pleasure and satisfaction while he shows off his good deeds and achievements in front of the people. In the implicit ostentation, though he does not show off his obedience in front of the people but performs it in secret, he secretly carves for people's recognition and honour. Even though it will be easy to save oneself from explicit ostentation, it will not be that simple to escape from implicit ostentation. Only those who have cleansed themselves from all traces of self-importance can win over implicit ostentation.

Your craving for getting people's attention to your distinctions betrays your insincerity in servanthood.

Even if the servant worships Allah in secret, his hidden desire to get people's attention and recognition for his distinction will spoil his sincerity in servanthood. People who are suffering from implicit ostentation cannot achieve absolute sincerity in their deeds because Allah knows all secret interests and intentions of their minds. He who fails to purge his deeds of all traces of ostentation cannot claim sincerity in his obedience.

Let Allah's taking notice of you outshine people's taking notice of you; and contemplate His treatment of you to outshine their treatment of you.

The servant should not allow himself to be led by people's comments and opinions about his deeds. Praise from people is harmful to spiritual health in the long run, as it will gradually take his focus away from Allah to people. He should train himself to concentrate on Allah, thinking about his status and image in front of Him so that he can outshine people's opinions about him. If his thoughts revolve round Allah, nothing from people will affect him. Just as the sun outshines the moon and all other satellites, Allah's light is capable of outshining all other sources of light.

Those who know Allah contemplate Him in everything;
those who are made extinct by Him are absent from
everything; and those who love Him prefer nothing to
Him.

The gnostic is so overwhelmed by divine light that they
find everything else unimportant and unworthy of existence.
For them, Allah's presence outshines everything in the world.
They celebrate the presence of Allah and the absence of the
entire world. They are passionate lovers of Allah and are so
deeply immersed in divine light that nothing in this world
can beguile or dupe them. Drunk with love for Allah, they are
unconscious of anything else.

Too close to see

You are veiled from Allah by His intense proximity to
you.

For a gnostic, Allah is too close to be seen. One cannot see
things if they are very close to his eyes. Just like one cannot see
his palm if he brings it closer to his eyes, he is unable to see his
Lord who is closer to him than anything else. Everything else
in this world is perceptible because they are kept in a certain
distance while Allah is too proximate to be seen.

He was veiled because of His intense presence and He
became unseen because of His great light.

Scientifically speaking, there are certain limitations
for human visibility. Human eyes are not capable of seeing
infrared and ultraviolet rays and whatever lie beyond them.
Allah's presence is so intense that feeble human eyes cannot

see Him. Human eyes are capable of seeing other things because their presence is not intense. Allah's light is so powerful that human eyes cannot see Him.

18

Human pleading versus divine blessings

Let not your pleading be the cause of His bounty because it will weaken your understanding of Him. Let your pleading be a means of expressing your servanthood and fulfilling (His) rights of lordship.

Allah is not bound to reply to any of the requests of his servants. Whenever He gives them anything He does so entirely of His own volition. Sometimes He gives them what they ask and sometimes what they do not ask. They cannot consider their asking and prayers instrumental in obtaining something from Allah because it amounts to questioning Allah's supreme authority and freedom. For a servant, supplication and prayers are means for registering servanthood and expressing humility in front of the Master. Through prayers he is merely administering the duties he owes to his Master and cannot impose his interests on Allah.

How can the latter (your pleading) be the cause of the former (His bounty)?

If a servant believes he is blessed by Allah on account of his request, it is equivalent to believing that his request could alter some of Allah's predestinations concerning his case. But Allah's blessings are predestined and nothing can alter them.

Far be it from the eternal decree to be dependent on causes.

Human reasoning is always incapable of explaining the logic behind Allah's eternal decrees. Neither his actions nor his words can alter Allah's decrees. Human intellect and reasoning are transient and new, while Allah's decrees are eternal and old.

His providence for you is not thanks to anything from you. Where were you when His providence approached you and His patronage came to you? There was neither sincerity of deeds nor (subsequent) states of mind in His eternity. There was nothing except pure grace and sublime bounties.

The word *"raḥmān"*, one of the most defining attributes of Allah, signifies the freedom and freewill of Allah in conferring His blessings on creatures. He blessed them with His bounties in this world irrespective of what they do in return. Their words and actions have no role in Allah's decision. Allah created them from nothingness, denying any role for them in Creation. He protected them in their embryonic stages, when they were not capable of doing anything, thereby denying them any claim to their birth. He nurtured them in their infancy and boyhood days, when they were not self-sufficient, denying them any say in their upbringing. He saves them from disasters and diseases and bestows on them other blessings irrespective of their obedience or disobedience, thereby denying them any influence in shaping their futures. No obedience, however sincere and pure it maybe, can influence Allah's sublimity.

He knew that servants would expect the appearance of the mystery of providence, so He said, "Allah will choose for His special mercy whom He pleases" (Qur'an, 2:105). And He knew if He left them like that, they would have abandoned deeds, depending too much on the Eternal, so He said: "Surely the mercy of Allah is nigh to those who do good" (Qur'an, 7:56).

Allah's freedom and volition makes His decisions far from being influenced by the deeds and words of creatures. He made His mercy dependent on His volition so that nobody can have any claim on it. But in order to avoid inaction and the dependence of man on the Eternal, He urged him to act, saying that His mercy is closer to those who are doing good deeds. Man is incapable of influencing Allah or winning His mercy with his good deeds, though Allah's mercy is likely to embrace only those who are doing good deeds.

Everything relies on the divine will which, in turn, depends on nothing at all.

Divine will is the supreme thing which cannot be influenced or altered by anything else. It is not subject to anything, while everything is subject to it. It is independent of everything, while everything is dependent on it.

19

Ashamed of asking

*Sometimes, good manners prompt them to keep away
from asking; they are confident of His providence and
too preoccupied with His invocation to ask Him.*

The gnostics who put their trust on Allah are ashamed
to ask Him. Since they are optimistic of Allah's providence,
they always resist the temptation to ask. They don't have any
misgiving about what is to come from Allah. They think it is
impolite to ask Allah for anything because they firmly believe
that Allah, who has created and nurtured them, knows better
the things they deserve and the opportune time it should
come.

*Only those who are susceptible to forgetfulness need
to be reminded; and only those who are prone to
carelessness need to be cautioned.*

Gnostics think that asking Allah for something is
equivalent to doubting His care. There is no need of reminding
Allah about His providence. Allah is not susceptible to
forgetfulness, so there is no need of reminding Him about His

works. And He is not subject to carelessness, so there is no need of cautioning Him.

The importance of being needy

The hour of need is the festive period for novices.

Since deprivation is a means of knowing Allah, a spiritual initiate considers it a better opportunity to improve his prospects of reaching Allah. When he feels he is in need of Allah's help he can better understand hids weakness and limitations and Allah's magnificence. One who is in need is better placed to understand Allah. The earlier he understands his need of Allah, the better he can improve his relationship with Him. He who does not feel that he is in need of Allah's help fails to understand his weakness and limitation and Allah's magnificence.

Sometimes you may get more benefit from the hour of need than from fasting and ritual prayers.

An initiate can better understand Allah in his deprivation than in his fasting and obligatory prayers. Fasting and ritual prayers are two ordinary means to understand and communicate with Allah. They are relatively less adventurous ways, as the initiate is not forced to acknowledge his lowliness and Allah's supremacy. Here an initiate has to be more dedicated and sincere in his activities in order to reach the destination. But deprivation is a special situation in which the initiate is forced to acknowledge his servanthood and Allah's dominance and facilitate his reaching Allah quickly.

The hour of need is a carpet full of gifts.

The hours of need provide a good opportunity for the initiate to mend his relationship with Allah. Though it may appear to be the most difficult situation in life, it is actually the most fertile period in life in terms of spiritual growth.

If you want to get gifts, you have to meet the criteria of (spiritual) poverty and deprivation—"Alms are only for the poor" (Qur'an, 9:60)

Only those who think that they are in need of Allah deserve His gifts. Those who pretend to be self-sufficient and think they can do without Allah do so at the risk of losing Allah's blessings. Alms are meant for the poor and not for the rich. Therefore those who want to get alms from Allah should meet the criteria of poverty and deprivation. It means the feeling that he is always in need of Allah is very important for an initiate to get more spiritual openings from Him. If he grows more self-sufficient and complacent about his potential to lead a spiritual life, it will adversely affect his dynamism and debilitate his quest for truth.

If you realise your attributes, He will help you with His attributes. If you realise your humility, He will help you with His glory. If you realise your incapacity, He will help you with His capability. If you realise your weakness, He will help you with His might and power.

Man can realise Allah's glory and omnipotence by understanding his own limitations and shortcomings. Compared to Allah's might and force, man's attributes are nothing. Man is asked to admit his defects and limitation so that Allah will help him understand His attributes.

※ ※ ※

20

Miracles are not a benchmark

Sometimes miracles are conferred on those whose righteousness is not up to the mark.

The true honour from Allah is the blessing of obeying Him and living as advised by His Prophet (ṣ). A spiritual aspirant is supposed to concentrate on perfecting his obedience rather than focusing on performing miracles and extraordinary things. Even those who are not perfect in their obedience can perform miracles and extraordinary things, while righteousness is the privilege of only those who can achieve perfection in their obedience.

Fruitful stability

The proof of Allah's putting you in a certain state is that He keeps you in it while it is fruitful.

Fruitful stability is better than futile changes. Stability can be more dynamic, while volatility may engender nothing. If Allah wants to bless His servant with a particular state of affairs, He will afford him stability and productivity in it. Allah will help him utilise this situation to the maximum and generate good results. An obedient servant will try to prove his efficiency and productivity irrespective of the situation he is placed in. He will seek consistency in his present situation instead of asking for better circumstances in his life.

Allah has likened the words of a true believer to a fruitful tree with its routs anchored deep in the soil and its boughs in the clouds. The tree is used as a beautiful metaphor for the synthesis of stability and fertility in the life of a true believer. This is followed by a description of an uprooted tree, which is employed as a metaphor for the floating, unproductive and rootless life a non-believer.

Boasting is meaningless

> *He who speaks under the auspices of his own virtues will be silenced by his wrongdoing to Allah, while he who speaks under the auspices of Allah's beneficence to him will not be silenced when he misbehaves.*

The significance of all good things done by a servant lies in his being blessed by Allah to do so. Therefore, he cannot boast of his virtues, which were only instrumental in implementing Allah's decision. His good deeds are not the products of his inherent virtue. If he were inherently virtuous, he could not have misbehaved and committed mistakes. His faults belie all his claims of inherent virtuousness. When he starts to boast of his grand achievements, his failures will laugh at him.

The power of divine light

> *The light of sages precedes their words so that their illumination is always followed by expression.*

The gnostic dedicates himself to Allah to be inspired by divine lights. His being illuminated by divine light is preceded by his words of supplication and prayer to Allah and is followed by his words of advice and guidance for people. He repeatedly begs Allah to equip his heart with light and wisdom so that he can guide people. Just as rain rejuvenates parched lands, the presence of divine light causes wise words and saintly expressions to sprout in their hearts.

Every utterance appears clad in the attire of the heart that it issues from.

Each and every utterance reflects the heart it sprouts from. Words uttered by a gnostic will be decked with the divine light that illuminates his heart and will have the power to influence hearts, to wet eyes and to bring about effective changes.

(Of the gnostics), he who is allowed to speak out is understood by people and his allusions are deciphered by them.

When the gnostic speaks on behalf of Allah, his words are properly understood by people. As he is speaking with the permission of Allah, he can easily convince them with the symbols and allusions he employs in his speeches. The processes of communication will be free from delay or any kind of interruptions, because they are wholeheartedly supported by Allah. His words will be more effective, as he is speaking under the auspices of Allah and for the cause of Islam but with scant regard for his personal interests and fame.

Obscured appearance

*Sometimes, inner realities, transcendental knowledge,
will make an obscured appearance if you are not
allowed to express them.*

Only those who can meet certain requirements of
sincerity and dedication are permitted to give expression to
their inner realities. The inner realities of those who are not
permitted to express them will find expression in a disguised
and somewhat eclipsed form. Since there will be neither divine
light nor sincere intention to improve the quality of their
dissemination, they will be rendered in poor light, so that they
will not influence people or change their minds.

Different streams of inner realities

*Their expression is either due to an ecstatic overflow or
for guiding a disciple. The former happens in the case
of beginners, while the latter happens in the case of
those who have acquired strength and are cognisant.*

In the case of an initiate, the expression of inner realities is
a spontaneous action which happens whenever they overflow
his heart. For a seasoned gnostic, expression is a means to
guide people and enlighten their minds.

*An expression is nutritious to the needy listeners, and
what you get from it is only what you are able to eat
thereof.*

Such expressions are spiritual provisions for the listeners
who imbibe from it what will help their spiritual sustenance
and support them throughout the journey. They inspire and
promote different people in different manners. Each traveller

derives from them what suits him best in his journey according to his capacity and requirements.

Sometimes he who is very close to an exalted position expresses himself about it, and sometimes he who has already attained it expresses himself about it. It becomes very confusing except to those who are insightful.

The expression varies in quality and nature according to the grade and position of the person. For those who are very close to Allah it is an expression of delight and enjoyment, while for those who have already reached Allah it is an assertive declaration of the truth. For an insightful listener there will be no difficulty understanding the differences between them.

Beware of smugness

Those who are still on the way should not give vent to their inspiration because it will demean their deeds in their hearts and prevent them from attaining sincerity with their Lord.

Those who are on the way to Allah are advised not to give expression to the divine inspiration they receive, as it may mislead them into self-importance. Instead of improving its quality with more dedicated efforts, he will be wasting time revelling in what he has achieved. He is not matured enough to understand its pitfalls, such as pride and arrogance.

Give Him His due

Do not stretch out your hand to take something from creatures if you do not understand that the (real) donor among them is your Lord. If you do so, you can accept what knowledge suits you best.

A spiritual novice is advised to handle with utmost care and caution what he receives from people. He is asked to abide by two basic principles while accepting anything from people. The first and most important principle is that he should believe Allah is the real donor of everything. If he gives credit to people, it will weaken his faith, integrity and credibility as a sincere servant. If he does not believe that Allah is the creator and real force behind it all, he will end up respecting and admiring people, according unnecessary importance to them. The second important thing is the choice he makes while receiving anything from people. He is advised to pick up only what suits his status and adds to his spiritual potential.

If the gnostic is reluctant to solicit his Lord for his needs, because he is satisfied with His will, then why is he not reluctant to solicit His creatures for his needs?

The gnostic is satisfied with Allah's will, however unpleasant it may be. Since he prefers Allah's will to his interest and needs, he is least bothered about what may happen to him. He is ashamed of submitting his needs to Allah because he thinks it is tantamount to betraying his trust and confidence. The gnostic is reticent about his personal interests and needs even in front of Allah, let alone in front of creatures.

21

Opt for the more difficult choice

If you are confronted with two alternatives, consider what is more difficult to you and choose it because nothing weighs on you except what is true.

What looks easy and comfortable for the self may not be good in the long run. On the face of it, the easier choice will be relaxing, while the difficult one will be less appealing. While opting for what appears more appealing to the self, the individual will be risking his capabilities to take up more challenging and rewarding tasks. The self may prompt him to opt for what is of lesser risk. But if he prefers to abide by the dictates of the self, it will weaken his power to prevail over a more difficult situation in the future and make him accommodate himself to reduced circumstances.

Supererogatory and obligatory deeds

A sign of one's adherence to passion is enthusiasm to carry out supererogatory deeds and laziness in doing obligatory deeds.

Obligatory duties such as the five daily prayers and the fast of Ramaḍān have been fixed by Allah for everyone while supererogatory deeds are left to man's choice and convenience. A true believer should be more enthusiastic about carrying out his obligatory duties than doing supererogatory deeds. He accords more importance to his duties fixed by Allah than what he prefers according to his whims and convenience. Laziness in doing obligatory deeds and enthusiasm about supererogatory deeds betray one's interest in what is comfortable for one rather than what is commanded by Allah.

He made (obligatory) deeds limited to specific times so that procrastination does not deflect you from them; and He made the time ample enough so that you have your share of choice.

Allah has fixed a timeframe for obligatory duties, such as the five daily prayers so that the servant cannot have a choice in its schedule. But He has allowed him enough time to do it within the prescribed timeframe, so that he was not denied his choice of timing.

He knows about the lethargy of servants in dealing with Him, so he made obedience to Him obligatory for them, herding them to obedience fettered by obligation. Your Lord is surprised to see people being herded to Paradise in fetters.

Allah created man to worship Him and made worship a condition for his entry to Paradise. But knowing man's laziness in worshipping Him, He made some forms of worship obligatory for him. Allah has forced His otherwise indolent servant to do certain forms of worship and forcibly drove him to obedience. Allah's obligation is like a chain dragging people to obligation. It is a weird spectacle to see people who are hesitant to go to Paradise being driven to it in chains.

He made it obligatory for you to serve Him. It means
He made it obligatory for you to enter His paradise.

By making certain forms of obedience obligatory for His servants, Allah intends to save them from disobedience in this world and from His punishment and Hell in the hereafter. Allah is so fond of His servants that He made it obligatory for them to escape the Hell and enter Paradise.

Those who consider it amazing that Allah saves them
from passion and takes them out of their forgetfulness
actually deem divine faculties feeble. And it is (only)
Allah who prevails over all things," (Qur'an, 18:45).

It is not difficult for Allah to save His servants from passions and forgetfulness. To consider it difficult for Allah is the same as suspecting Allah's divine power and attributes.

Blessings via trials

Sometimes   darkness   may   envelop   you
in order that He make you aware of the
importance of His graces He conferred on you.

Man is created weak and is not able to understand the true value of the blessings Allah has bestowed on him. Man is so ungrateful to Allah that he does not appreciate, Allah while he is still enjoying His graces. Sometimes Allah tests him by covering him in darkness so as to make him aware of His blessings.

He who does not know the importance of (divine) graces in their presence does know it in their absence.

Man is prone to disregarding Allah's graces while he is still enjoying them. But he will reflect on and understand their true value when he no longer enjoys them. Allah, who knows best this ingratitude inherent in man, sometimes takes away His blessings and makes him ponder what he really lost.

Be careful of glitz and sweets

Do not let the abundance of graces dazzle you, so that they keep you away from your obligation of gratitude, because it will make your rank plummet.

If a servant allows himself to be lost in the glitter and glamour of divine graces rather than concentrating on his duty of thanking Allah, it will badly affect his spiritual status. He will become accustomed to such a meaningless and superficial life without being able to explore the true pleasure obtained by carrying out his obligatory duties. The more Allah graces him with His blessings, the more seriously he should engage in improving his relationship with Him. The deeper he indulges in the enjoyment of worldly achievements, the more superficial his relation with Allah will be.

When sweet passions reign over your heart it will result in chronic diseases.

Just as the excessive consumption of sweets increases the possibility of being afflicted with diabetes, excessive indulgence in the sweetness of this world will make the heart vulnerable to various incurable diseases. A true believer will not allow too much worldliness, as he is aware of its lethal force. He is afraid of any enjoyment that may enfeeble his spiritual health and corrode the immunity of his heart against evil forces.

Passion cannot be driven out from the heart except by an alarming fear or an impatient desire.

Fear of Allah and an intense affection for Him are the two means by which a spiritual aspirant drives out the evil persuasions of passion from his heart. Fear of Allah and His punishment will dissuade him from the allures of passions, while an intense craving for Allah will deter him from doing anything that Allah does not like.

Get rid of hypocrisy

Just as He does not like deeds tinged with hypocrisy, He does not like a heart tinged with hypocrisy. He does not accept deeds tinged with hypocrisy, while He does not come near a heart tinged with hypocrisy.

A true believer is more careful of purging his heart and deeds of any trace of hypocrisy. Hypocrisy is the rival of a believer, as it pollutes all good deeds and takes the heart out of its sheen of faith. Those who crave for Allah's appreciation cannot allow his deeds and heart to be contaminated with hypocrisy.

❈ ❈ ❈

22

Two types of divine light

(There are two types of lights:) Lights that are allowed to reach and lights that are allowed to enter.

When divine light reaches the surface of his heart, the believer starts to feel the presence of Allah inside him. He becomes conscious of Allah and the hereafter. Understanding the significance of belief in Allah and the hereafter, he divides his time both for himself and for Allah and works both for here and the hereafter. He will try to give both this world and the hereafter their respective dues. When divine light enters the heart, it makes a big change, persuading the believer concentrate only on Allah and the hereafter. Once the light enters the heart, this world and all its riches become irrelevant for him and he forsakes working for them.

Making way for the light

Sometimes lights come to you and, finding the heart stuffed with earthly figures, go back to where they came from.

Divine light will hesitate to enter the heart if it finds it is too preoccupied with earthly concerns. The light cannot feel at home in a heart which is teeming with worldly preoccupations.

Empty your heart of vicissitudes to fill it up with intuitions and mysteries.

The spiritual aspirant is asked to stuff his heart with gnostic intuitions and mysteries in order to facilitate the arrival of divine light. A barren and rocky land is not able to receive and store rain water, while a fertile land imbibes rain water and decks itself with sprouts and blooms at will.

Do not think His present comes tardily; but rather think your receptivity is slow.

The believer is asked to prepare his heart for receiving divine light. He should blame none other than himself if its arrival gets delayed. If divine light is slow to come it is not because Allah sent it late but because of the problems in his own receptivity.

Obligations to time

It is possible to delay discharging time-bound obligations; but it is not possible to delay discharging the obligation inherent in every moment, because there is no moment without your having a new obligation or a more serious matter from Allah. How can you discharge in this moment another moment's obligation when you have not discharged obligations from Allah in it?

Time-bound obligations can be delayed or postponed to some other occasion. But it is not possible to delay the obligation inherent in each and every moment in life.

As man is created to obey Allah, no moment of his life is exempted from obligation. Apart from time-bound obligations, such as the five daily prayers and fasting, he has to discharge one kind of obligation or other in each and every moment of his life. If he is enjoying happiness and welfare in life, his obligation is to express thanks and gratitude to Allah; if he is facing some trials and tribulation in life, his obligation is to exhibit patience. If he is lucky enough to obey Allah, his obligation is to ensure his total absorption in sincerity and dedication; if he commits any crime, his obligation is to repent immediately and to ask Allah's forgiveness. These obligations inherent in each and every moment in his life cannot be postponed to another occasion because he is not free from such obligations at any moment in his life.

There is no substitution for the part of you life that has gone by, while what you have achieved from it is invaluable.

Time is very precious and there is no substitute for each moment that ticks away. Man is neither the creator nor the preserver of time; though he is given a certain amount of freedom to spend his gift as he likes, he has no authority at all concerning his past and future. For a believer, life is an opportunity to celebrate his servanthood. As the Messenger of Allah (ṣ) said, each moment in which a servant could not remember Allah, is a great loss and cause for regret in his life. The value of each second is beyond the comprehension of the human being. He does know the true value of a moment, which he either squanders or utilises.

Be a slave only to Him

You have not loved anything without being a slave of it. But Allah does not want you to be a slave of someone else.

The lover wants to do anything to please the beloved. His top priority is winning the beloved's heart by hook or by crook. Allah does not want His servant to be a blind lover of anything else, lest something other than Him is his first priority. One who blindly loves this world and its material riches cannot prioritise Allah's commandments. If he does not love Allah, he will seek to find shortcuts to bypass Allah's rules to attain what he loves most.

Allah does not benefit from obedience

Neither does your obedience benefit Him nor does your disobedience harm Him. It is only for your benefit that He commanded certain things and proscribed certain others.

Allah is so exalted and dignified that He is in no way affected by either the obedience or disobedience of servants. It is only for their benefit that He laid down rules and regulations for them and sent servants and holy books to preach to them from time to time.

If someone draws closer to Him, it does not add to His power; and if someone withdraws from Him it does not diminish His power.

Neither the obedience of the servants increases the sublimity of Allah nor does their disobedience decrease it. Allah's power is so exalted that nothing in the world can impinge on it.

23

Reach Him through contemplation and knowledge

Your reaching Allah is your reaching knowledge about Him. Otherwise, Allah is beyond being reached and beyond reaching anything.

Allah is in such an elevated position that no one can unite with Him. A servant's union with Allah means his union with knowledge of Him. He understands Allah through understanding His attributes. Each will form his opinion and visualise the image of Allah according to the knowledge he got about Allah. The better he knows Allah, the more transparent and accurate his vision of Him will be.

Your proximity to Him is that you can contemplate His proximity (to you). Otherwise, how on earth can you attain His proximity?

The servant is not allowed physical proximity to Allah, though he can mentally come closer to Allah through constant contemplation and supplication. A believer attains the nearness of Allah through his contemplation of Him. The growth and development of this attachment with Allah is based on the intensity of his meditation and the enlightenment he derived from it.

Gradual acclimatisation

In the time of illumination, the truths come altogether, and their explanations come only after retention. "So when We promulgate it, follow its recital. Nay more, it is for Us to explain it (and make it clear)" (Qur'an, 75:18-19).

When divine illumination dawns on the heart of the believer, it cracks open a world of inner realities inside him. This will be followed by his gradual acclimatisation to the particulars of the new world introduced to him. Anchored deep in the material world, the servant cannot undergo a sudden metamorphosis. Therefore it takes time for him to prepare himself for the alteration.

When divine inspiration, do away with your routine. "Kings, when they enter a country, despoil it" (Qur'an, 27:34).

Once blessed with the divine inspiration, the servant is no longer his older self. It ushers in fresh ideas and new methods to his life and takes him to a totally different world. It librates him from the shackles of indolence and purges him of all sorts of dirt.

Inspiration is powerful

Since inspiration comes from the presence of the Omnipotent, nothing can resist it without being torn apart. "Nay, We hurl the truth against falsehood, and it knocks out its brain, and behold, falsehood perishes!" (Qur'an, 21:18).

Divine inspiration comes with such a massive and volcanic force that it overpowers all recalcitrant forces. It will tear to shreds all efforts of resistance. As it comes for a complete overhaul of the self, it does not tolerate any trace of opposition.

He is apparent in everything

How can Allah be concealed by something if He is apparent and visible in what He has been veiled.

Allah's presence is manifest in everything in the universe because He is the creator and cherisher of everything. If He is manifest in everything, nothing can hide Him and, moreover, nothing can be used to hide Him.

Leave to Him the reward

Do not despair if your deed, wherein you could not perceive a divine presence, is accepted. Sometimes, He will accept your deed the reward of which you cannot perceive right away.

Man is not an infallible judge of his own deeds. Sometimes he cannot perceive the real value of his acts. If he fails to notice divine presence in his deeds, he cannot jump to the conclusion that they are not worthy acts.

Do not attach credibility to an inspiration whose reward you do not know. The real purpose of clouds is not to bring rain but to yield fruits.

The true intention of divine inspiration is to effect a complete change in the personality and attitude of the servant. It is supposed to replace all his bad habits with good ones and take his heart closer to Allah. But if the advent of divine inspiration is not accompanied by a sea change for the better in the life of a servant, it serves no purpose at all; it will be deluding him on the pretext of inspiring him. The servant should stay away from entertaining such a treacherous stimulation which camouflages itself with the attire of divine inspiration, deceiving him.

Seek Him and only Him

Do not seek the persistence of (divine) inspirations after their lights have dawned on you and their mysteries deposited in you, because in Allah you have one who enables you to dispense with everything, but nothing enables you to dispense with Allah.

Once divine light has served its purpose of enlightening the heart with divine secrets, there is no point in expecting its continuity. Its abrupt cessation or absence need not necessarily disappoint a servant who relies on Allah. He should believe that trust in Allah can compensate for the loss of anything in life, however great and beloved it maybe, but nothing is capable of compensating for Allah's care and support. Man can do without anything if Allah is with him; but he cannot do without Allah even if the whole world extended all support to him.

Your seeking the persistence of something other than Him is proof that you have not found Him. Your alienation because of losing something other than Him is proof that you have not reached Him.

One who knows and understands Allah well will never be disturbed by the absence or presence of anything. He will not seek the persistence of anything other than Allah because he knows that nothing other than Him is meant for eternal persistence. If one feels disturbed by the loss of anything in the world it means he has not properly understood Allah.

24

Divine presence is paramount

Divine grace, however diverse its manifestations maybe, is attained through contemplating and drawing near to Him; Suffering, however diverse its manifestations maybe, is due to His veil. The veil is the cause of the suffering, while the perfection of grace is achieved through looking at the countenance of Allah, the Generous.

Divine grace has a lot of manifestations. A wide variety of happiness and enjoyment created by Allah for His servants in this world and the hereafter demonstrates this diversity. But the most important of all divine graces is the opportunity to contemplate and feel the presence of Allah. Without this, all other graces are not worth enjoying. Even in the hereafter, where the believer is offered a number of heavenly blessings, seeing Allah is the most important of all.

This is not different in the case of suffering both here and in the hereafter. The most tragic of all this suffering is the denial of Allah's presence. A veil that hides Allah's presence or sight is the most painful of all suffering in the life of a servant.

*What prevents you from attaining insight causes the
worries and grief in your heart*

The denial of inner light, which is attained through
contemplating Allah, is the bitterest and most tragic thing in
the life of a believer. There is no point at all in obtaining all
means of happiness without experiencing Allah's presence.

*His providing you with what is sufficient, and denying
you what makes you exceed the bounds, means that
He has perfected His grace on you.*

Allah perfects His graces on a servant when He blesses
him with sufficiency. The possession of too much wealth and
other material riches does in no way symbolise the perfection
of divine grace.

The happier, the more tragic

*Let your happiness about something be less, so that
your grief over it will be less.*

A true believer will consider this world a temporary
arrangement and all its gains a transient phenomenon.
Therefore, he will not attach too much importance to the
moments and objects of happiness in this life. He knows well
that nothing is going to stay for long, so he will be ready to
forsake whatever he achieved at any time. Such a prudent and
wise approach will help the believer accept any loss or defeat
without lamentation.

If you do not want to be isolated, do not take up the reins of a post that is not lasting.

Power and position are so alluring that once enjoyed, their charms are not likely to leave man. But since no position is permanent, the pleasure accompanying them is also not to stay for a long time. So it is wise not to take charge of any position so that you avoid the grief at the time of relinquishing it.

If the beginning made you desirous, the end will make you isolated. If the exteriors draw you near to it, the interiors prevent you from it.

Though the power and prestige appear to be tempting at the beginning stage, their intransience and instability are the causes of grief and isolation. Attraction in the beginning will summarily give way to disappointment and frustration. Its exteriors are inviting, while its interiors are admonitory. Most people are gullible about the glitter and glamour of its exteriors, and only those who are able to see its interiors can understand and avoid the pitfalls.

He made the world a place of vicissitudes and a mine of dirtiness to make you repugnant to it.

The allure of this world is really misleading, and the trials and tribulations of it reveal its real nature. Allah created adverse circumstances, such as poverty, squalor, natural disasters and diseases, in this life to distract people from it. They are admonitory signs which prevent man from indulging too much in worldly riches. One who contemplates the reality behind it will be ready to sacrifice this problematic life, which is fraught with all sorts of adversities, for an enduring and more rewarding world.

A blessing in disguise

Since He knows that you will not accept mere advice, He makes you sample the tastes of this world so as to ease your separation from it.

Allah knows that mere advice is not sufficient to rescue people from being misguided to the traps of this world, so He made them taste the suffering of this world to facilitate their distraction from this world. Viewed in this perspective, adversities and setbacks in life are really divine blessings to rescue the servants from the snare of this world.

The most useful knowledge

Useful knowledge is knowledge whose rays dawn on your heart and take your heart out of its covering.

The purpose of knowledge is to unveil the opaque covering of the heart, letting the rays of light enter it. If knowledge is really useful, it will take the heart closer to Allah and distract it from material interests. Knowledge which in no way serves this purpose is totally useless.

The best knowledge is knowledge which is accompanied by fear (of Allah).

It is the scholars who fear Allah most among His servants, as the Qur'an makes clear. But the best knowledge of a scholar is what generates piety and fear of God in him. Therefore true knowledge and fear of God are always complementary to each other.

Knowledge, if it's coupled with fear (of Allah), is in your favour; if not, it is against you.

Knowledge has no value at all if it is not accompanied with the fear of Allah. Knowledge which does not add to piety and fear of God is not only useless but also harmful, as it will generate pride and self-importance in the heart. The purpose of knowledge is to liberate man from the restricted spheres of his self to the wider horizon of Allah, the Creator.

If it pains you to see people not coming to you or mistreating you, take recourse to your knowledge of Allah. If knowledge of Him does not satisfy you, then your suffering from dissatisfaction with knowledge of Him is greater than your suffering from pain caused by people.

If a servant is blessed with divine knowledge, no mistreatment or discrimination from creatures can disappoint him. He will not be affected by any negligence from people, because he pays no heed to anything other than Allah and believes that even if the whole world were against him, Allah would be there to help and support him. The more the world neglects him, the more he neglects the world, and the more it laughs at him, the more he laughs at it. Whenever the world tries to defeat him, his faith and piety help him to defeat the world.

If the servant is not satisfied with knowledge of Allah, then nothing can satisfy him. This dissatisfaction will be bitterer than any other dissatisfaction caused by people.

Turn only to Him for solace

He made you suffer at the hands of people so that you will not depend on them for repose. He wanted you to be troubled by everything so that nothing will alienate you from Him.

Allah has made the believer suffer at the hands of people so that his mind will find solace only in Him. It makes him believe that only Allah can save him from what His creatures do and encourages him not to give this world undue importance. It is because Allah wants you to seek His help, and His help only, that He made everything trouble you.

If you know that the Devil will not forget you, do not forget the one who holds your forelock.

If the Devil always pursues man to distract him from Allah, as he himself promised, Allah will also be there holding man's forelock and saving him from the snarls of the Devil. A believer who pins his faith and trust on Allah need not fear any harm from the Devil.

He made the Devil your enemy to take you to Him through him; and he stirred up your soul against you so as to make you constantly submit to Him.

The enmity of Satan and man is a blessing in disguise. The presence of this strong and crafty opponent forces man to seek Allah's protection. Because of this enmity, man will be always vigilant and precautious. He will be careful to be constantly in the company of Allah lest the enemy my hit anytime.

Allah created some enemies for man within himself they are his own passions, which distract him from his objectives. These enemies within will create a lot of problems for him, so that he will be forced to seek Allah's help against them.

In short, Allah created both external and internal enemies for man to warn him about the necessity of fortifying himself with the help and support of Him.

25

Humility

He who attaches weight to his humility is really proud, because humility emanates only from a sublime state. Therefore whenever you attach weight to your humility, you are really proud.

A humble man is not the one who thinks, when he humbles himself, that he is above what he did; on the other hand, the humble man is the one who thinks, when he humbles himself, that he is below what he did.

Humility is a sublime human attribute exclusive only to those who own a great mind and good dispositions. Arrogance betrays one's weakness and ignorance, while humility reflects one's strength and greatness. The humbler one becomes, the loftier one grows; the more arrogant one becomes, the lower one plummets. Humility is the hallmark of those who recognise their shortcomings as human beings and understand the glory and power of Allah. They will never hold themselves in high esteem because they know that they are of lesser importance compared to the full-scale control of Allah over their lives. This recognition leads them to an exalted and distinguished position compared to those who give unnecessary importance to their doings. Therefore, a humble servant is really proud of his recognition while an arrogant one is oblivious of his ignorance.

Real humility emanates from the contemplation of His sublimity and the enlightenment of His attributes.

It is only the contemplation (of His) attributes that can take you away from (your own) attributes.

Understanding the sublimity of Allah and the greatness of His attributes are the essential prerequisites for achieving humility. Pondering over Allah's attributes is an effective way to understand the meekness of human attributes. Through constant contemplation of Allah's attributes, the servant can liberate himself from the influence of his attributes, which will create hindrances on his way to spiritual enlightenment.

The adoration of Allah

The believer is too engaged with praising Allah to praise himself and is too engaged with the rights of Allah to remember his fortunes.

A perfect believer will not extol himself because he does not see anything worth praising in himself. He thinks that if everything that he can stake a claim for is created by Allah, then praising himself instead of Allah is meaningless and a total waste of time and energy. He will also be aware of the temporariness of his fortunes and their dependence on Allah, so he will not waste his time thinking about them, preferring instead to perform his duties to Allah.

The lover does not want a reward from his beloved, nor does he claim any objective. The true lover is the one who is generous to you and not the one who you are generous to.

If the devotee is really sincere in his adoration of Allah, he will not expect or seek any reward or compensation for his worship. If he loves Allah truly, he should not expect anything in return because a true lover gives everything at his disposal, expecting nothing in return. As a true lover who will sacrifice everything to please his beloved, a dedicated servant will strive to do everything he can to please Allah, regardless of what Allah will give him in return.

The journey of the soul

Had it not been for the domains of the self, the journey of the wayfarers could not be successful; for there would neither have been a distance between you and Him that you traverse in your journey nor a barrier between you and Him that will be effaced by your reaching Him.

The journey to Allah mainly includes crossing the temptations of the self. The distance between the servant and Allah is littered with obstacles of the self—its passions and cravings—without conquering which reaching Allah will ever remain a pipedream. On the other hand, if there is no selfish interest for men, the distance between the traveller (servant) and destination (Allah) will cease to exist. And without a destination to cross, the question of a journey will never crop up. But Allah created the impediments of the self on the way to Him to maintain the distance so that the servant can reach the destination with the sweat of his own brow.

The synthesis of physical and spiritual dimensions

He placed you in the intermediary world between His Dominion (the visible world) and His Kingdom (the invisible world) to teach you the majesty of your position among His creatures and that you are a jewel hidden in the oysters of His Creation.

Man is a unique blend of physical and spiritual dimensions. Unlike other creatures, he was created with both earthly and heavenly elements. Allah has positioned man in the intermediary world between the world of Dominion (*mulk*) and the world of Kingdom (*malakūt*), thereby enabling him to acquire the qualities of creatures in both worlds. The world of Dominion (*mulk*) is the visible world whereas the World of Kingdom (*malakūt*) is the invisible world. Being earthly and heavenly at times, he is equipped with the spiritual attributes of angels and the physical features of creatures on the earth, like animals and plants. Allah has blessed man by bestowing on him the natures of all creatures. He is intelligent and obedient like angels, and arrogant and belligerent like devils. He also exhibits various animal features, such as courage, lust, shrewdness and deception. Allah has honoured him with all these blessings and assigned to him a difficult task that even the angels cannot carry out. These extra features make man distinguished from all other creatures.

The universe surrounds you only in terms of your corporeal existence, but it does not surround you in terms of your spiritual existence. He who exists in

the universe is imprisoned by his surroundings and is confined in the temple of his body, so long as the domains of the invisible world are not opened to him.

Man cannot surpass this world with his physical features only. Had it not been for his spiritual dimension represented by the soul, he would have been restricted to this world. His corporeal existence is restricted to this world, while his spiritual existence helps him transcend the limitation of this world and soar into the invisible domains. Only when he enjoys access to the invisible world with the help of his spiritual dimension, he can liberate himself from the constraint of his corporeal existence. Like the wings which help a bird fly heavenward, the soul helps man to take his body away from the cage of this world to the freedom of the invisible world.

You shall remain with the creatures till you contemplate the Creator; and once you contemplated Him, the creatures shall belong to you.

As long as man does not understand his spiritual potentials, he shall remain one among many of the creatures in the world. Only those who employ their distinctive spiritual skills and contemplate the Creator can stand out from other creatures. The range of their difference from other creatures varies commensurate with their efficiency in utilising their spiritual dimension. The power and intensity of their contemplation take them closer to Allah and give them command over other creatures. In a more advanced stage, they, with the permission and approval of Allah, will at times take control of creatures and ask them to do certain things, just as prophets and saints did on several occasions.

Getting rid of human attributes is not a prerequisite
for attaining constant sanctity. Sanctity is analogous to
the light of the sun during the day. It appears in the
horizon but is not part of it. Sometimes, the sun of His
attributes rises the night of your existence, while on
other occasions, He takes it back from you and takes
you back to yourself. So the sun is neither from nor to
you; but it is something that comes on you.

The sanctity that allows man to enter the divine domain does not necessitate the deterioration of human attributes. Man cannot cast aside his humane attributes and corporeal existence, however spiritually exalted he maybe. Even while basking in the glory of divine light, his human attributes will remain intact. The dawning of divine light in his heart is similar to the appearance of the Sun on the eastern horizon. Just as the sun which appears on the horizon is not owned by the horizon, the divine light which radiates the heart of a believer is not owned by the believer. When the divine light dawns on the heart of a believer, it liberates him from all the deformities and deficiencies of his corporeal existence. But when Allah takes the light back, the heart will be left alone with its old deficiencies. It means the divine light is not a permanent attribute of man, nor does it enjoy a permanent stay in the human heart; but rather it comes as a visitor who makes frequent visits if the host is really worth a visit.

Two types of journey

He alludes with His creatures to the existence of
His names, with His names to the existence of His
attributes and with His attributes to the existence

of His being, because it is impossible for attributes to stand alone. To those who have reached a state of spiritual ecstasy (jadhb), He reveals the perfection of His being; and then He takes them to the contemplation of His attributes. Afterwards, He takes them to the reflection of His names and then to the contemplation of His creatures. But as for those who are still on the way (sālikīn), the journey will be in the reverse order. Their end will be the beginning for the ecstatic, while the end for the latter will be the beginning for the former, albeit not in the strict sense of the word. Sometimes they meet on the way, one ascending and the other descending.

An initiate begins his journey to Allah from the creatures which take him to Allah's names first, then to His attributes and then to His existence. All the creatures in the world allude to a creator, a benefactor, a cherisher and a lot of other names that Allah calls Himself. From these names one can understand Allah's attributes. But the attributes which cannot stand alone should naturally point to the existence of Allah, who is the possessor of all these attributes.

But those who have reached a state of spiritual ecstasy (*jadhb*) will begin their spiritual journey in a reverse order. Allah will first introduce them to His existence, from where He gradually takes them to His names and creatures. The initiate begins his journey from creatures, where one who experiences spiritual ecstasy will end ones journey. The former begin from where the latter end and vice versa; and sometimes both of them will meet on the way, when one is ascending and the other descending.

Visible and invisible worlds

The worth of the lights of hearts and of secrets is known only in the invisible world (the hereafter), whereas the lights of the sky do not appear only in the visible world (in this world).

The true worth of divine light and its fruits can only be measured in the invisible world (the hereafter) because the yardstick of the visible (corporeal) world is too weak to judge divine light. In the pure light of the visible world, they may not appear worthy of note but their true value will be understood only in the invisible world. The visible world will understand and recognise only material lights, such as the light of stars, which emanate from and end in this world without entering the invisible spheres.

Getting the fruits of obedience in this world is glad tiding of the rewards due to its performer in the hereafter.

Allah will give His obedient servant a glimpse of the reward awaiting him in the hereafter through some early blessings in this world. It means Allah makes him continue in this way with satisfaction and enjoyment.

Seeking reward

How can you seek reward for a deed which He donated to you? Or how can you seek reward for the sincerity which He gifted to you.

The ability and desire to worship Allah is one of the most important divine blessings. If all good deeds done by man are due to this divine generosity, he has no right to seek reward for them. Man can seek Allah's reward only if he has done something good for Allah through his worship. But it is Allah who has done something good for him by enabling him to be an obedient servant. If the ability to worship Allah itself is a divine blessing, there is no point in seeking a reward for that.

Divine light and invocation

There are people whose lights precede their invocations, and some others whose invocations precede their lights. That is, there are invokers who invoke to illuminate their hearts, and invokers who became invokers because they illuminated their hearts.

Those who have reached a state of spiritual ecstasy (*jadhb*) are the exclusive ones who achieve divine light without invocation. In their spiritual journey, divine light comes first, followed by invocation (*dhikr*). They invoke because their minds are illuminated with divine light. But the case of initiates is different. They have to invoke before attaining divine light. The purpose of their invocation is to illuminate their hearts with light. The former get divine light as an honorary reputation, while the latter accomplish it with their efforts.

Invocation becomes manifest through internal contemplation.

For both the ecstatic and the initiate, invocation is an outward expression of inward contemplation of Allah, though the intensity of their contemplation differs according to their respective status and position.

Witnessing

Before asking you to bear witness (to Him), He made you witness. The outward signs be speak His divinity, while the heart and secrets have realised His oneness.

Before asking man to bear witness to His existence through worship and dedication in this world, Allah has made him witness His oneness and glory during the Conference of the Souls (the meeting of the souls in *ʿālam al-arwāḥ*) before their arrival to this world. At that time, his outward faculties spoke of His divinity, and the heart and innermost secrets had realised His unity and oneness. The meeting of the souls and their recognition of Allah's divinity are gestures with a lot of symbolic significance. It stands for man's secret acknowledgement of Allah's divinity and oneness. Man, however arrogant and profane he might be in this world, recognised and acknowledged Allah with both his soul and body earlier. The only thing he is asked to do in this world is to be true to his early words of acknowledgement.

Three phases of invocation

He honoured you with three gifts: 1) He made you invoke Him, and had it not been for His grace, you would not have deserved the flow of invocation in you; 2) He made you remembered by Him because He confirmed His association with you; 3) He made you remembered by those with Him and confirmed His grace upon you.

There are three stages of evolution in the invocation of a devoted servant. Throughout the process, Allah helps the devotee to improve his performance and reach the next stage. The first stage begins with the invocation of Allah, wherein Allah rescues the servant from all diversions and helps him concentrate on remembering and invoking Him. In the second stage, Allah makes him remembered along with Him as a confirmation of His association with him. It means in this stage, the servant will be known as a saint of Allah and people will consider him a true guide and a means to attain spiritual solace. In the third and final stage, the servant will be elevated to the most exalted position, wherein the servant will be remembered by Allah. It is the consummation of the invocation and the fulfilment of Allah's promise "Remember me and I will remember you".

A long life

Some lives are long in terms of years but short in terms of results, while others are short in terms of years but abundant in terms of results.

The value of human life depends on its productivity rather than on its longevity. For each human being, life is a divine gift with which he is sent to this world. Man is also endowed with a lot of faculties, through the effective application of which he will be able to make better use of the gift of life. Those who can efficiently use their faculties do not want long lives to prove their mettle whereas those who fail to apply their skills will be wasting their lives even if they are blessed with long lives. The fruitful moment of an efficient man who utilised his skills is better than the whole life of an inefficient one whose faculties were disabled and whose innate skills were put in cold storage.

He who has been blessed in his life will get in a shorter span of time gifts from Allah neither words can express nor symbols can allude to.

Those who are blessed by Allah can utilise their time and faculties effectively so that they can achieve in a shorter span of time what others fail to achieve in many years. A moment blessed by Allah will be more fruitful and creative than a whole life devoid of divine blessings. With the blessings of Allah one can achieve in a night what the efforts of a thousand months cannot attain.

It would be really disappointing if you were unable to move to Allah while free of (worldly) responsibilities, or if you were unable to travel to Allah while having few obstacles.

Worldly responsibilities may distract a servant from Allah. People who are preoccupied with the concerns of their daily bread will get lesser time to spend for Allah. The more concerned he is with this world, the less interested he will be in spiritual pursuits. But those who are blessed with enough of this world and relieved of worldly responsibilities will have no more obstacles to prevent them from travelling to Allah.

However if one still fails to make inroads to Allah, even after he was blessed with material riches, it shows his moral deterioration.

Contemplation

Thought is the journey of the heart in the realms of the vicissitudes (of creatures).

Meditation or thought is likened to a floating ship over the waves of the vicissitudes and alterities of life. Thought is a process which awakes the mind to the realities of the things around and eventually to the presence of their omniscient and omnipotent Creator. Thought helps one to reflect on the triviality and transience of all creatures compared to the power of the Almighty. Thought is also instrumental in keeping man afloat in murky waters littered with all sorts of worldly problems.

※

Thought is the lamp of the heart. If it goes away, the heart will be devoid of light.

Thought plays an important role in the sustenance of man's spiritual health. Without meditation to fuel the light of the heart, the heart will be full of darkness. Thought is an active process which keeps the mind dynamic, vigilant and creative in many respects.

※

There are two types of thoughts: thought about belief and faith and thought about contemplation and vision. The first is the case for reflective thinkers, while the second is the case for contemplative and visionary thinkers.

The thought or contemplation of those who are in spiritual ecstasy will be different from that of those who are still journeying to Allah. The former consider thought a product of their contemplation and vision, while the latter consider it a means of reiterating their belief and faith. The latter are reflective thinkers who gradually reach Allah from His creatures, while the former are visionary thinkers who start their contemplation from Allah and finally reach creatures.

Appendix 1
The First Letter

In a letter to some of his friends, he wrote:

Beginnings are the places wherein the ends are revealed. (Beginnings cast light on the ends). He who begins with Allah will also end up with Him. The things that occupy you are the ones which you love and rush to; the things you turn away from are the ones which were not preferred by you. Whoever is certain that Allah seeks him will be sincere in his pursuit of Him, and whoever knows that everything is in Allah's hands has agreed to put his trust in Him. It is inevitable for the pillars of this existence to crumble and for its honours to be stripped away.

The wise one is he who is happier with what is eternal rather than with what is transient. His light rises and is followed by the coming of good tidings.

He turns away from this world, pays no heed to it, spurns it altogether. He does not make it his nation or turn it into a home. But in it he pursues his ambitions towards Allah and walks in it seeking His help to reach Him. The riding mount of his determination is restless and continues its journey till it kneels down in the holy presence and on the carpet of intimacy—the place of dialogue, meeting, companionship, discussion, contemplation and observation.

So the (divine) presence has become a nest for their hearts, a nest they seek refuge and dwell in. When they descend to the heaven of responsibilities and the earth of fortunes, they do so with permission, consistency and deep certitude. They did not come down to the responsibilities with improper behaviour or forgetfulness, nor did they descend to the fortunes with passion and enjoyment. On the contrary, they entered them by Allah, for Allah, from and to Allah.

Say, "'O my Lord! Let my entry be by the gate of truth and honour, and likewise my exit by the gate of truth and honour,' (Qurʾan, 17:80) so that when You make me enter I will look at Your might and strength, and when You make me get out I will submit and surrender to You. Give me helpful evidence which will help me and help (others) through me but will not help against me. It will also help me against self-importance and will do away with me from the circles of my senses."

Appendix 2
The Second Letter

In another letter to his friends, he wrote:

If the eye of the heart sees Allah alone in His blessings, the law stipulates that it is necessary to thank His creatures (also).[1]

In this, people are of three classes. The first one is the absent-minded one who is immersed in his oblivion. Though the realms of his senses are strong, his inner vision stands blurred. So he sees the munificence coming from creatures and does not consider it coming from the Lord of the universe.[2]

The second one is the man of spiritual reality, who by contemplating the real King is absent from creatures. The effects are non-existent to him because of his contemplation of the Cause of the effects. He is a servant brought face to face with the Real, the grandeur of which is manifest in Him. He is a wayfarer who has mastered the course of his path. But

---

1.   In a broader spiritual perspective, all blessings are from Allah and there is no role for any creature. Therefore only Allah is entitled to be thanked. But the law (*sharī'ah*) stipulates that creatures should be given their due of thanks. If a man gets a benefit from a fellow human being, it asks him to thank Allah and the man who was instrumental in bringing it.
2.   It maybe either out of belief in which his idolatry is apparent or out of dependence in which his idolatry is invisible.

he is so submerged by lights that creatures are imperceptible to him. His inebriety outshines his sobriety, his union his separateness, his extinction his survival and his absence his presence.

The third and the best of all is a servant who drinks and becomes more sober. The more absent he is, the more present he becomes. His union does not prevent him from his separateness nor does his separateness prevent him from his union. His extinction does not block his survival nor does his survival block his extinction. He behaves justly to everyone and gives everything its due.

Abū Bakr al-Ṣiddīq said to 'Ā'ishah, when her innocence (in a defamation case against her) was revealed by the Prophet (ṣ); "O 'Ā'ishah, be grateful to the Messenger of Allah!" She replied, "By Allah, I will thank only Allah!" Abū Bakr informed her about the more appropriate course of action-the position of survival, which requires considering creatures. Allah says, "Give thanks to Me and to your parents" (Qur'an, 37:14). The Messenger of Allah (ṣ) said, "He who does not thank mankind does not thank Allah." But 'Ā'ishah was denuded of her senses, was away from creatures and could not contemplate anyone except the One, the Omnipotent.

Appendix 3
The Third Letter

When he was asked whether *the eyes delight* referred to in the saying of Allah's Messenger (ṣ) "The delight of my eye is in the prayers" is exclusive to Allah's Messenger (ṣ), he said:

The eye's delight obtained through contemplation is commensurate with knowledge about the contemplated thing. No one's knowledge is like that of Allah's Messenger (ṣ) and the delight of anyone's eye is not like that of Allah's Messenger (ṣ).

We mean that he get his eye's delight in his prayers through contemplating the majesty of the contemplated because he indicated this by saying "in the prayers". He did not say "by the prayers" because his eyes would not be delighted by anything other than his Lord. How could it be otherwise when he points to this position and directs others to realise it with his words "Worship Allah as if you see Him." It would be impossible for him to see Him and contemplate someone else along with Him.

Someone might say, "The eye's delight can be by means of prayers because the prayer is a favour from Allah emerging from Allah's blessings". Therefore, how can one not be pleased with it and how can one not have the eye's delight by means of it? For Allah says, "Say, In the bounty of Allah, and in His mercy—in that let them rejoice" (Qur'an, 10:58).

But you must know that the verse implies a reply to those who ponder over the secrets of the statements. Allah says "in that let them rejoice" and not "in that you rejoice, Muhammad." It means "Say to them, 'Let them rejoice by means of generosity and kindness', but let your rejoicing be with Him who is kind." In another verse, He says, "Say, 'Allah'!Then leave them to plunge in vain discourse and trifling" (Qur'an, 6:92).

Appendix 4
The Fourth Letter

In another letter, He wrote to some of his friends:

People are of three categories with respect to (their responses to) the advent of blessings:

(The first one) rejoices in blessings, not with respect their conferrer or creator, but considering his enjoyment in them. He belongs to the forgetful people about whom Allah's words ring true: "Until, in the midst of their enjoyment of Our gifts, on a sudden, We called them to account" (Qur'an, 6:44).

(The second one) rejoices in the blessings, considering them blessings from Him who sent them. Allah's words ring true about him: "Say, 'In the bounty of Allah and in His mercy—in that let them rejoice. That is better than the (wealth) they hoard'" (Qur'an, 10:58).

(The third one) rejoices in Allah. Neither the external pleasure of the blessings nor their inner graces distract Him. His looking to and concentration on Allah distracts him from any other thing. Only Him does he contemplate. Allah's words "Say, 'Allah!' Then leave them to plunge in vain discourse and trifling" (Qur'an, 6:92) rings true about him. Allah revealed to David, "O David, say to the truthful, 'In Me they should rejoice; and My invocation they should enjoy!'

May Allah make your and our rejoice with Him and with the satisfaction that comes from Him. May He include us in those who understand Him and not in those who are forgetful; and with His grace and munificence may He take us in the course of the pious.

※ ※ ※

Appendix 5
Intimate Discourses

And he said:

My God, if I am poor in my affluence, how should I not be poor in my poverty?

My God, if I am ignorant in my knowledge, how should I not be the stupidest in my ignorance?

My God, the differences in Your planning and the swift advent of Your preordination prevent Your gnostic servants from finding comfort in (worldly) gifts and from despairing of You during trials.

My God, I am the source of everything related to my meanness and You are the source of everything related to Your generosity.

My God, You made kindness and compassion to me Your attributes even before the existence of my weakness. Then why do You prevent me from them after my weakness?

My God, if virtues come from me it is because of Your grace; so it's up to You to bless me. And if vices come from me it's because of Your justice; so it's up to You to produce proof against me.

My God, how can You entrust me with myself when You are in charge of me? And how can anyone do harm to me when You are my protector, or how can I grow disappointed when You are affectionate to me? I make my need of You a means to seek access to You. How can I seek access to You by means of something by which it is impossible to reach You. Or how can I complain to You about my situation when it is not unknown to You? Or how can I render myself to You in my words, which stem from and go to You? How can my hopes go astray if they are headed for You? Or how can my situations not be good if they are based on and headed for You?

My God, how compassionate You are towards me despite my great ignorance, and how merciful You are to me despite my vile deeds.

My God, You are very close to me, while I am very distant from You.

My God, You are so merciful to me. So what veils me from You?

My God, I know from the diversity of creatures and from the vicissitudes of life that You want me to understand You in everything so that I will not ignore You in anything.

My God, whenever my ignobility makes me dumb, Your munificence makes me articulate. Whenever my attributes disappoint me, Your grace makes me optimistic.

My God, if one's virtues are really evils, then why can one's vices not be really vices? If one's realities are really affectations, why can one's affectations not be really affectations?

My God, Your effective verdicts and Your forceful will make the articulate speechless and the important trivial.

My God, my dependence on acts of obedience I built and situations I erected was often razed by Your justice. But it was your grace that liberated me from it.

My God, You know that although my obedience has not persisted as a resolute action, it has persisted as love and firm will.

My God, how can I be firm while You are the Omnipotent, or how can't I be so while You are the Commander.

My God, my vacillation among creatures makes my destination farther. So connect me with You through a service that guides me to You.

✻

My God, how can one take as a proof of You something which depends on You for its existence? Will anything other than You manifest something that You do not have so that it becomes Your manifestation? When did You become so absent that You are in need of a proof to bear evidence of You, and so distant that it's the creatures themselves that show the way to You.

✻

My God, blind is an eye that cannot see You monitoring it, and unsuccessful is the deal of a servant who has not won a share of Your love.

✻

My God, You have ordered me to go back to creatures. Return me to them, clad in the cloths of lights and with the guidance of inner vision, so that I will return to You from them as I entered You from them, with my secrets being guarded from looking at them and my determination so high that it does not depend on them. You are, truly, powerful over everything.

✻

My God, I submit my lowliness in front of You and unveil my situation to You. And from You I seek to join You and by means of You I seek proof of You. Guide me to You with Your light and keep me with sincere servanthood in front of You.

My God, teach me from the knowledge of Your treasury and safeguard me with the secret of Your guarded name.

My God, make me discern the realities of those who are closer to You and make me tread the path of those who are in spiritual ecstasy.

My God, make Your planning dispense with my planning and make Your preferences for me dispense with my preferences; make me stay along with the centre of my needs.[1]

My God, take me out of my self-humiliation and cleanse me of my doubts and polytheism before I join my grave. I beseech Your help, so help me. Only You I trust, so do not entrust me (to someone else). Only You I ask, so do not turn me down. Your grace I crave, so do not reject me. To You I belong, so do not banish me. At Your door I stand, so do not cast me off.

My God, if Your pleasure is too holy to have any cause from You, how can it have a cause from me? If You are in person independent of any benefit coming to You, why should You not be independent of me?[2]

My God, fate and divine decree have triumphed over me, and desire with its strong passions hold me prisoner. Be my

---

1.   A request for being always in need of Allah.
2.   There is no point in distinguishing the causes and effects in Allah's existence. Allah does not require a cause for His existence from Himself, let alone causes from creatures.

protector so as to help me and help (others) through me.
Enrich me with Your graces, so that I will be too contented to
ask You. You illuminated with lights the hearts of Your saints
so that they knew You and avowed your oneness. You kept the
vicissitudes away (from them) so that only You they loved and
only in You they took refuge. You entertained them when they
were isolated by the world. You guided them till the landmarks
were visible for them. What did he who has lost track of You
manage to get? And what is there to lose for one who has
found You? Truly he went astray who has considered someone
else a substitute for You; and truly he is lost who seeks to stray
from You.

My God, how can one pin his hope on someone other than
You when You have not cut off Your benevolence? How can
one beseech someone other than You when You have not
changed the habit of bestowing bounties?

O He who makes His beloved ones taste the nectar of His
intimacy so that they stand in front of Him with admiration,
O He who clothes His saints in the attire of reverence to Him
so that they stand exulting in His magnificence, You are the
invoker before all invokers (You remember them before they
remember You); You are benevolent before servants turn to
You; You are the most munificent giver before seekers beseech
You; and You are the great benefactor who, in exchange of
what You have given, seeks a loan from us.

My God, seek me with Your grace so that I will join You, and
draw me (to You) with Your blessings so that I will draw closer
to You.

My God, my hope will not be separated from You even if I disobey You, just as my fear will not leave me even If I obey You.

My God, the world pushed me to You, and it is my knowledge about Your benevolence that made me stand in front of You.

My God, how can I be disappointed while You are my hope, or how could I be disgraced while I am still dependent on You?

My God, how can I attach glory to myself while You have positioned me in lowliness, or why should I not attach glory to myself if You have associated me with You? Why should I not be in need (of You) if it is You who placed me in poverty, or why should I be in need if You have enriched me with Your generosity? There is no God but You. Since You made Yourself known to everything, nothing is ignorant of You. You made Yourself known to me in everything, so I have seen You visible in everything and visible to everything.

O He who ascends to His throne with His mercy, making the throne invisible in His mercy just as the whole worlds become invisible in His throne, You have effaced creatures with creatures and obliterated vicissitudes with the spheres of lights surrounding them.

O He who is veiled in the canopy of His glory so that eyes cannot see Him, O He who illuminates with the perfection of beauty whose greatness is realised by the secrets, how can You be hidden if You are visible, or how can You be absent when You are the monitor of the present.

Made in the USA
Middletown, DE
15 September 2023

38568534R00099